Disney · PIXAR

COCO

THE OFFICIAL COOKBOOK

Disney · PIXAR

COCO

THE OFFICIAL COOKBOOK

By Gino Garcia

TITAN BOOKS

LONDON

CONTENTS

Guarniciones 81
Accompaniments

Dulces y Postres 91
Sweets and Pastries

Pan Dulce 103
Sweet Breads

Bebidas 117
Beverages

In late 2017, I was in Mexico City when *Coco* premiered, and it quickly became Mexico's highest-grossing film at the time. For many of us, *Coco* felt like a breakthrough in Hollywood storytelling. It was original and playful but still honest and bittersweet. The filmmakers beautifully reimagined the real-world city of Santa Cecilia and the Land of the Dead, both recognizable places that felt familiar onscreen.

We all watched the story of Miguel Rivera, a young boy who dreams of becoming a musician, unfold despite his family's generations-old embargo on music. In pursuit of his ambitions, he accidentally finds himself on a literal and figurative quest to reconnect and reconcile with the past. His adventures in the Land of the Dead—a glittering metaphor of an afterlife—tell a story that is both specific and universal.

Within weeks of *Coco*'s release, I saw it three times in theaters: once in Spanish and twice in English. By the end of the year, I listened to "Remember Me" enough times to make it my #1 Most Listened To Song of 2017. As someone from a generational Mexican-American family, I found that *Coco*'s storytelling resonated with me. I saw myself in the ways people casually slip in and out of untranslated Spanish. As a musician and dancer, I even related to Miguel's drive to pursue a creative path. And like Miguel, I, too, set forth on a quest to recover my own lost roots.

Now, as a chef and culinary ethnographer, sharing food is my favorite means to this end. I've met countless people and scoured stacks of books to better understand the histories and culinary traditions of Mexico. With the help of other trained chefs, writers, talented home cooks, and historians on both sides of the border, I've constructed bridges to connect the many worlds I inhabit. This cookbook is a product of that intentional and ongoing work.

The recipes in this book reflect the geographic and cultural influences depicted throughout *Coco*. Many of the recipes are pulled directly from the film; others add layers to a world it created. I've included a mix of dishes that are beloved standards of Mexican cuisine, such as *Pozole* and *Chiles Rellenos*, as well as some lesser-known and contemporary dishes, such as *Nicuatole* and *Tamal de Fresa*.

By cooking through this curated collection of memories and recipes, my hope is that we remember the parts of the film we fell in love with while immersing ourselves in an expansive and dynamic cuisine. May these recipes help you create beautiful plates of food that are as multidimensional and meaningful as Miguel's journey.

—Gino Garcia

INGREDIENTS GUIDE

The recipes in this book feature ingredients such as chiles, herbs, and spices that might be more readily available in some areas of the country than others. Some recipes offer substitutions for certain specialty items, but many of them can be found at online retailers and in some local ethnic markets. If you keep your kitchen stocked with these Mexican ingredient staples and become acquainted with how to use them, you'll be set up to make many of the dishes in this book and take advantage of limitless other cooking opportunities.

Beans

One of the most emblematic ingredients of Mexican cuisine, beans are a fixture at every dinner table. The recipes in this book reference mostly pinto beans, white beans, and black beans. Cooking with dried beans is more economical and gives the ingredients more depth of flavor. Canned beans can be substituted, although the flavor of the final dish can vary.

Chiles

The recipes in this book use chiles in three forms: dried, fresh, and canned. Most of the chiles are easy to find in grocery stores or online.

DRIED CHILES

Shop for chiles that are pliable and deep colored. Brittle dried chiles are older and less flavorful. Store chiles in an airtight container at room temperature for several months, or extend their shelf life by keeping them in the freezer.

- GUAJILLO: Mild and fruity flavor, a versatile and foundational chile for many sauces

- ÁRBOL: Very spicy, slightly nutty, and acidic, used for its peppercorn-like heat
- MORITA: Smoky, but fruitier than a chipotle chile, with medium heat
- ANCHO: Mild to moderate heat, with a deep red color and a raisin-prune flavor
- PEQUIN: Very small, fruity, and spicy, used commonly in sauces and for making chile flakes
- MULATO: Key ingredient in making some moles, similar to an ancho chile but with more heat and a smoky flavor
- PASILLA: Smoky and fruity flavor similar to a raisin, less sweet than an ancho chile

FRESH CHILES

Buy chiles that are brightly colored, firm, and unwrinkled. To tame the heat, remove the seeds before cooking and serving.

- JALAPEÑO: Medium heat, vegetal and bright flavor
- SERRANO: More heat than a jalapeño, crisp and grassy flavor
- POBLANO: Large, thick-walled green chile with mild to no heat, commonly used for charring and stuffing

CANNED CHILES

- CHIPOTLES EN ADOBO: Contains a ripened and smoke-dried jalapeño chile that marinates in a spiced sauce. Both the chiles and the sauce are used in ingredients.

Chocolate

Mexican chocolate is a medium-dark chocolate that is roasted and coarsely ground. It is seasoned with cinnamon, coarse sugar, and sometimes chiles and nuts. The flavor is more intense and less processed than other types of chocolate sold in stores, making it perfect for *champurrado* and *mole*. Because of its unique flavor and texture, Mexican chocolate cannot be substituted for other types of chocolate in recipes.

Cinnamon

Most of the tightly rolled sticks we buy in grocery stores are actually a kind of cinnamon called cassia. This variety can taste harsher and almost spicy, and it is not a good ingredient for adding to a blender. Mexican cinnamon (also called *canela*) and Ceylon cinnamon are milder and more floral. The bark is longer and thinner and flakes easily, making it safe to use in a blender for sauces.

Epazote

This pungent herb grows like a weed in warm and dry climates. Its medicinal aroma can be a bit curious, with notes of mint and oregano. It mellows out when cooked and gives many Mexican recipes an unmistakable earthy flavor. *Epazote* is typically added to long-cooking beans and soups, but it can also be used as a fresh garnish in quesadillas and savory salsas.

Garlic

Unless otherwise noted in a recipe, all garlic cloves should be peeled from their skins before prepping. Unpeeled garlic is necessary for charring; the cloves are peeled when cool enough to handle, to infuse sauces with toasted garlic flavor. Avoid pre-minced jarred garlic, which tends to have an acidic and fermented flavor.

Masa

Dried corn is treated with pickling lime (cal) using a process called nixtamalization. This allows the corn to be milled into a soft and pliable dough (*masa*) for making infinite Mexican dishes. Masa for tortillas is ground more finely, whereas masa for tamales is coarse and produces a fluffier texture. The two types of masa are not interchangeable.

Freshly milled masa can be found at some Latin grocery stores and specialized small businesses. Fresh masa is a ready-to-use dough that comes in two forms: *masa preparada*, which is seasoned with spices, and *masa quebrada*, an unseasoned dough that you can customize yourself. Corn masa flour (*masa harina*) is easily available in most grocery stores and can be substituted, but it is not as flavorful or soft in texture. You must add water to masa harina before using it in recipes.

Onions

I prefer white onions for their cleaner, milder flavor. Because they are higher in water content than other onions, white onions are crunchier and hold their structure better when cooked. Yellow onions can be substituted for white onions, but they are sweeter and can become mushy when cooked. Red onions are more assertive in flavor when raw, but they become sweeter when cooked. For this reason, a red onion is not an ideal substitute for a white onion.

Oregano

Despite sharing a similar-sounding name, Mexican oregano comes from a different plant family than the oregano grown and used widely in the Mediterranean. Mexican oregano has more citrus and anise notes, whereas Mediterranean oregano can be mintier, earthier, and more pungent. Both types can be used in any recipe, although, in my opinion, dried marjoram makes a better substitute for Mexican oregano.

Piloncillo/Panela

This brown, unrefined cane sugar is sold either in the shape of a cone (*piloncillo*) or as a disk (*panela*). It has a rich, molasses-like flavor and is used in both sweet and savory dishes. For some recipes, the entire cone or a large chunk can go directly into the pot. For specific measurements of piloncillo, grate the sugar on the large hole side of a box grater. Dark brown sugar can be substituted in equal parts, with some flavor and consistency differences.

Tomatoes

Most recipes in this book use Roma (plum) tomatoes, which are ideal for a couple reasons. When charring, their longer shape is convenient for blackening all sides evenly. Roma tomatoes are also more dense and do not have as much watery pulp, which makes them perfect for flavorful and substantial sauces. If ripe tomatoes are not available, canned tomatoes make great substitutes. For charred sauces, choose canned fire-roasted tomatoes; for most other uses, whole canned tomatoes are good substitutes.

MENUS

La Tamalada

A *tamalada* is a gathering where friends and family come together to assemble, cook, and eat tamales. Making tamales together is one way to remember and connect to our past and present while also creating memories that last into the future. Here are a few tips for organizing your tamalada:

PREPARE THE MASA

- To offer both vegetarian and meat options, prepare multiple batches of masa that can be used for filling.

- If you are buying masa harina (dried corn flour), use the masa intended specifically for making tamales, which has a coarser texture than masa for tortillas.

- If you are buying fresh masa for tamales, called masa quebrada, you also have the option of buying masa preparada, which is already seasoned with spices and ready to use. If you buy the unprepared masa, you can add your own spices and flavorings.

PREPARE THE FILLINGS

- Whatever fillings you choose, be sure they are cold when you assemble the tamales. This ensures that the fillings are easier to portion. Fillings are also a good task to have guests prepare at home before attending the tamalada.

- For smaller tamaladas, choose two to three filling types—at least one meat and one vegetarian—to make the work more manageable.

- Suggested tamale filling recipes include:

  - Rajas con Queso, page 46
  - Frijoles con Queso, page 46
  - Pollo en Mole Rojo, page 47
  - Pollo en Salsa Verde, page 47
  - Picadillo, page 47

START THE ASSEMBLY LINE

- Assign at least one person for each of the following steps in the process: scraping the masa onto the husks, portioning the filling onto the masa, and folding the husks and placing the tamales into the steamer pot.

- Focus on finishing one filling at a time so you can keep track of the tamales. You don't want guests to be surprised by a *Pollo en Salsa Verde* tamal when they were expecting a vegetarian one.

COOK THE TAMALES

- Depending on how many people are at the tamalada and how many tamales are being made, I recommend using either one very large steamer pot or multiple smaller pots. If you expect to make a lot of tamales, consider asking your guests to bring their own steamer pots.

- Tamales can be stacked in a pot either with the open ends facing up or horizontally. The latter technique allows for more tamales to fit into a pot, but you must also pinch and seal the open end of each tamal so that the filling does not spill out while cooking.

ADD ACCOMPANIMENTS FOR TAMALES

- Salsa Roja, page 43
- Salsa Verde, page 74
- Chiles en Escabeche, page 87
- Cebollas Encurtidas, page 89

OFFER BEVERAGES TO ENJOY BEFORE, DURING, AND AFTER THE TAMALADA

- Champurrado, page 123
- Ponche, page 125

Snackworthy Bites at the Sunrise Spectacular

Small nibbles to enjoy at a larger-than-life show or cuddled up on the couch with a movie at home.

Favors and Main Dishes for a Fiesta

In *Coco*, the town of Santa Cecilia, like many towns in Mexico, features a lovely plaza where people gather to hear music, shop, and connect with each other. These classic flavors and aromas transport you to the hustle and bustle of the Plaza.

La Taquiza Mexicana

This homey, buffet-style meal is perfect for more casual gatherings. All it takes is a few simple taco fillings, warm tortillas, and a table full of loved ones to make this meal complete.

Large-Batch Cooking

These recipes are easily scalable and technically simple, and they could feed a small town, if needed.

Ensaladas y Antojitos

SALADS AND APPETIZERS

Xec

Yucatecan Jicama and Citrus Salad

Difficulty: Easy
Prep Time: 15 minutes
Yield: 6 to 8 servings
Dietary Notes: Vegetarian, Dairy Free, Gluten Free

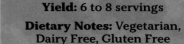

From tart and floral limes to honey-sweet tangerines, this savory and crunchy salad puts citrus fruits front and center. Miguel likes oranges the most, and he brings them to share with Mama Coco when he updates her on the day's events. She doesn't always remember everything he says (or who Miguel is), but he still loves to spend time with her.

1 pound jicama, peeled and cut into ¼-inch cubes

Juice of 2 limes (about 2 tablespoons)

¼ cup orange juice

¼ cup grapefruit juice

1 tablespoon honey

½ habanero chile, finely diced (or ½ teaspoon cayenne powder)

½ teaspoon kosher salt, plus more to taste

2 large navel oranges, peeled and separated into segments, halved

3 mandarins or tangerines, peeled and separated into segments

1 pink grapefruit, peeled and separated into segments, halved (see note)

2 tablespoons chopped cilantro

1. Add the cubed jicama to a large bowl and toss with the lime juice to prevent browning. Cover the jicama with plastic wrap, and refrigerate while preparing the rest of the ingredients.

2. To make the dressing, combine the orange juice, grapefruit juice, honey, chile, and salt in a small bowl, and whisk the ingredients together. In a large bowl, add the oranges, mandarins, and grapefruit; then pour the dressing over the fruits, add the chopped cilantro, and mix well. Let sit for at least an hour to let the flavors meld before serving.

NOTE

Alternatively, to wow your guests, you can supreme the grapefruit.

1. Cut both ends off the grapefruit.

2. Stand up the fruit on one of its flat ends and cut down along the rounded side with your knife to remove a piece of the rind and pith. Repeat until all the rind and pith are removed.

3. To remove the segments of flesh, cut along the interior of each membrane and pull the segments out. Make sure you're working over a bowl to catch all the juice.

4. Squeeze out the remaining juice in the membranes and discard.

Garden Salad with Creamy Pepita Dressing

Mama Imelda's companion, Pepita, is an imposing yet beautiful jaguar spirit guide in the Land of the Dead. In the Land of the Living, Pepita takes on the smaller and more docile (although no less powerful) form of a lovable cat. Pumpkin seeds are a companion of the pumpkin, an icon in Mexican culinary heritage, and deliver outsized flavor and richness to many traditional dishes, from moles and puffed seed candies to this creamy salad dressing.

Difficulty: Easy
Prep Time: 20 minutes
Yield: 4 servings
Dietary Notes:
Vegetarian, Gluten Free

SALAD

4 cups mixed salad greens, washed and dried

12 cherry tomatoes, halved

2 to 3 small radishes, sliced thinly

1 Persian cucumber, sliced thinly

CREAMY PEPITA DRESSING

¼ cup pepitas, toasted

3 tablespoons chopped parsley

1 garlic clove

Juice of 1 lime (about 1 tablespoon)

3 tablespoons extra virgin olive oil

½ teaspoon kosher salt

¼ serrano chile, seeded

¼ cup plain Greek yogurt

TO MAKE THE SALAD:

1. In a large mixing bowl, add the greens, cherry tomatoes, radishes, and cucumber; set aside.

TO MAKE THE DRESSING:

2. In a food processor, add the pepitas, parsley, garlic, lime juice, olive oil, salt, chile, and yogurt; blend until it looks like a very smooth purée, stopping every few seconds, as needed, to scrape down the sides of the bowl.

3. Drizzle ½ cup of the dressing on top of the salad, and gently toss to coat. Add more dressing or seasoning to your liking.

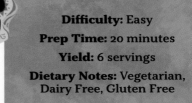

Difficulty: Easy

Prep Time: 20 minutes

Yield: 6 servings

Dietary Notes: Vegetarian, Dairy Free, Gluten Free

Shredded Carrot and Beet Salad

Miguel has only one thing on his mind while running through the crowded cemetery: Get Ernesto de la Cruz's guitar from his mausoleum and compete in the talent contest. Somehow he isn't distracted by the beautiful red and orange glow of marigold flowers left at all the gravesites. You certainly will not ignore this stunning salad that brings those colors to your plate with the help of vibrant raw carrots and beets.

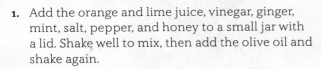

Juice from 1 large orange (about ¼ cup)

Juice from 2 limes (about 2 tablespoons)

1 teaspoon apple cider vinegar

1 teaspoon grated fresh ginger root

2 sprigs fresh mint, leaves removed and sliced thinly, plus more for garnish

1 teaspoon kosher salt

¼ teaspoon freshly ground black pepper

1 teaspoon honey

2 tablespoons extra virgin olive oil

4 large carrots, grated

3 red beets, grated

1. Add the orange and lime juice, vinegar, ginger, mint, salt, pepper, and honey to a small jar with a lid. Shake well to mix, then add the olive oil and shake again.

2. Add the carrots to a mixing bowl and toss with half the dressing. Add the beets to another mixing bowl and toss with the remaining dressing.

3. To plate, place a portion of the carrots next to a portion of beets, and garnish with the remaining mint before serving.

Ensalada de Nopal

Grilled Cactus Salad

Difficulty: Easy
Prep Time: 20 minutes
(plus 1 hour wait time)
Cook Time: 10 minutes
Yield: 4 servings
Dietary Notes: Vegetarian,
Gluten Free

Nopales (prickly pear cactus) are native to Mexico, so it is common to find them cut into strips and added to stews or even juiced for a nutritious beverage. This salad is one of the more popular dishes that lets this vegetable shine. Full of texture and flavor, it can accompany any main dish.

2 large cactus paddles, spines removed (see How to Prepare Nopales)

2 tablespoons kosher salt, divided

1 large Roma tomato, diced

½ white onion, diced

1 serrano chile, finely diced

1 avocado, diced

⅓ cup queso fresco

1 tablespoon lime juice (about 1 lime)

2 tablespoons olive oil

½ teaspoon dried Mexican oregano

1. Place the cactus paddles on a clean plate and sprinkle about 1 teaspoon of salt on each side. Let rest for 1 hour, then thoroughly rinse the cactus paddles under cold water until they no longer feel slimy.

2. Preheat a grill pan or outdoor grill on medium-high heat. Sprinkle the prepared nopales with a generous pinch of salt on all sides; cook them for 8 to 10 minutes, turning halfway to cook evenly. Remove the nopales from the heat and let them cool.

3. In a large bowl, combine the diced tomato, onion, chile, avocado, and queso fresco. When the nopales are cool enough to handle, dice them and add them to the bowl with the other ingredients.

4. In a smaller bowl, whisk together the lime juice, olive oil, remaining salt, and Mexican oregano. Drizzle the dressing over the salad, lightly toss, and then serve. The salad can be refrigerated and enjoyed slightly chilled.

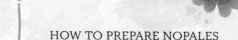

HOW TO PREPARE NOPALES

To remove the spines, hold the cactus at one end and run a sharp paring knife against the grain of the spines on both sides of the cactus. Cut away the outer ¼-inch edge of the cactus and 1 inch from the base of the cactus where it was pulled from the larger cactus plant.

Papaya with Coconut and Chile

Difficulty: Easy
Prep Time: 10 minutes
Yield: 4 to 6 servings
Dietary Notes: Vegetarian, Gluten Free

Buttery papaya has a subtle melonlike sweetness that is usually enjoyed with breakfast. *And* it is beloved enough by Frida Kahlo to be in her new performance piece for the Sunrise Spectacular. Inspired by her revolutionary spirit, this recipe gives new and exciting flavors to a tropical fruit worthy of center stage.

1 medium papaya, peeled, seeded, and cut into wedges

Juice of 2 limes (about 2 tablespoons)

2 teaspoons honey

½ serrano chile, thinly sliced (optional)

½ teaspoon kosher salt

¼ cup unsweetened coconut flakes, toasted

1. Put the papaya wedges on a large plate, and set aside.

2. In a small bowl, mix the lime juice, honey, sliced chile, and salt, and drizzle the papaya wedges with the dressing. Sprinkle the coconut flakes over the papaya, or roll the wedges in the coconut; then serve.

Elote Callejero

Mexican Street Corn

Difficulty: Easy
Prep Time: 20 minutes
Cook Time: 10 minutes
Yield: 4 servings
Dietary Notes:
Vegetarian, Gluten Free

Miguel and his family discover that Ernesto de la Cruz isn't the person they thought he was. His true villainous ways are revealed to the entire audience at the Sunrise Spectacular, who cheer uproariously when Pepita throws him out of the theater. A single audience member returns to his seat with a treat similar to this delicious and iconic Mexican street food and asks the person sitting next to him, "What did I miss?"

4 ears fresh corn, shucked

1 tablespoon vegetable oil

1 teaspoon kosher salt

¼ cup Mexican crema

¼ cup mayonnaise

½ lime, zest and juice

1 garlic clove, grated

½ cup Cotija cheese, finely crumbled, plus more for garnish

¼ cup cilantro, leaves and stems finely chopped, plus more for garnish

1 teaspoon cayenne chile powder

Hot sauce of your choice, for garnishing

Lime wedges, for garnishing

1. Preheat an outdoor grill or grill pan to medium heat. With clean hands or a brush, rub each ear of corn in the vegetable oil and a generous pinch of salt. Place the corn on the grill and cook until it is evenly charred on all sides, about 10 minutes.

2. While the corn is cooking, mix together in a large mixing bowl the crema, mayonnaise, lime zest and juice, grated garlic, Cotija cheese, cilantro, and chile powder. When the corn is finished cooking, remove it from the grill; roll each cob in the crema and cheese mixture, and then transfer it to a platter. Garnish to taste with the remaining cheese, cilantro, and hot sauce, and serve with a lime wedge.

Vuelve a la Vida

Spicy Seafood Cocktail

Difficulty: Easy
Prep Time: 10 minutes
(plus at least 1 hour wait time)
Cook Time: 5 minutes
Yield: 4 to 6 servings
Dietary Notes: Dairy Free

With every passing moment in the Land of the Dead, Miguel is becoming more *muerto* himself. He must find a way to return to the Land of the Living before it's too late! Perhaps this popular Mexican seaside appetizer, which translates to "Come Back to Life," would've helped Miguel. Its intense and spicy flavor can certainly help revive you when you're feeling a bit muerto.

1 pound mild white fish filets, such as sea bass or halibut, cut into ½-inch pieces

Juice of 14 limes (about 2 cups)

3 garlic cloves, 2 smashed and 1 finely grated

2 teaspoons kosher salt, plus more to taste

1 pound large shrimp, peeled and deveined

2 Roma tomatoes, finely chopped

1 to 2 jalapeños, finely chopped

1 small white onion, finely chopped

½ cup cilantro, chopped

1 cup ketchup

1 tablespoon Worcestershire sauce

1 to 2 tablespoons vinegar-based hot sauce

1 tablespoon distilled white vinegar

2 teaspoons sugar

1½ teaspoons dried oregano

¼ cup extra virgin olive oil

1 pound lump crabmeat

¼ teaspoon freshly ground black pepper

1 large ripe avocado, halved, pitted, and diced

Corn tostadas or saltine crackers, for serving

1. Add the diced white fish and lime juice to a large mixing bowl. Gently mix, cover with plastic, and let marinate in the refrigerator for at least 1 hour, or up to 3 hours.

2. Fill a large pan with water, 2 smashed garlic cloves, and a generous pinch of salt, and bring to a boil on high heat. Prepare a small bowl with ice water, and set aside.

3. Add the shrimp to the pan; then reduce the heat to medium and cook until the shrimp just starts to turn pink, about 1 minute. Use a spatula or slotted spoon to immediately transfer the shrimp to the ice water, and let cool for 2 minutes. Drain the shrimp, pat dry with a paper towel, and chill in the refrigerator.

4. In a large bowl, mix together the grated garlic, tomatoes, jalapeños, onion, cilantro, ketchup, Worcestershire sauce, hot sauce, white vinegar, sugar, oregano, and olive oil.

5. Remove the marinated white fish from the refrigerator and add the fish to the bowl with the vegetables, along with the cooked shrimp, crabmeat, and 1 cup of the lime juice marinade. Gently mix, then season with 2 teaspoons of kosher salt and the black pepper. Taste and adjust seasonings, as needed.

6. To serve, portion the seafood to a small bowl; then top with diced avocado and either tostadas or saltine crackers on the side.

Masa

FRESH AND DRIED
CORN DOUGH

Difficulty: Medium

Prep Time: 10 minutes

Cook Time: 30 minutes

Yield: About sixteen
6-inch tortillas

Dietary Notes: Vegan,
Dairy Free, Gluten Free

Tortillas de Maíz

Corn Tortillas

Making tortillas is part recipe and part intuition gained from practice. Everyone can master the various steps of making tortillas—from how much liquid to add to the masa (dough), to how to shape and cook them to perfection. Freshly milled masa is used for the Rivera family's daily preparation of tortillas. This recipe gives methods for using both fresh masa and masa harina (dried corn flour), which can be found in most grocery stores.

FRESH MASA

4 cups (about 2 pounds) masa preparada or masa quebrada (see Ingredients Guide, page 8)

Water, as needed

SPECIALTY TOOLS

Tortilla press

Tortillero (tortilla warmer), optional

1. The masa should have the consistency of a stiff cookie dough. If it is crumbly or grainy, add water (1 tablespoon at a time) and thoroughly massage it into the dough. Form 16 golf ball–size balls and cover them with a damp dish towel to prevent them from drying out.

2. Warm a nonstick pan or a griddle over medium heat.

3. Prepare a quart-size resealable plastic bag or parchment paper to cover the tortilla press: If you're using a resealable plastic bag, cut the bag along the sides so that it makes two symmetrical halves; if you're using parchment paper, cut pieces large enough to fit the tortilla press—about 6 to 8 inches for standard tortilla presses. This step is necessary to prevent the uncooked masa from sticking to the press.

4. Lay one piece of cut plastic on the bottom plate of the tortilla press, and place a masa ball on top of the plastic in the center. Place the second sheet of plastic on top of the masa ball, and press down firmly until the tortilla is about ⅛ inch thick.

5. Open the press and remove the flattened masa with the two sheets of plastic: Place it in the palm of one hand and, with the other hand, gently peel off the top sheet of plastic. Flip it over to the other hand, and carefully peel off the other plastic sheet. If the tortilla tears or is stuck to the plastic, scrape off the masa and start over. If the masa is too sticky, let it sit for a few minutes, to dry up any excess moisture. If it is too crumbly, add a sprinkle of water to moisten it.

6. Gently place the raw tortilla in the preheated pan. Let the tortilla cook, untouched, for about 30 to 45 seconds on one side. When the edges start to turn up slightly and the tortilla moves more easily in the pan, flip the tortilla to the other side and continue cooking for 45 seconds to 1 minute.

7. Lastly, flip the tortilla back to the original side and cook for 30 to 45 seconds. At this point, the tortilla might inflate. Put the finished tortillas in a *tortillero* (tortilla warmer) or a deep bowl lined with a clean dish towel, to keep them warm until you're ready to serve them.

Masa Harina
Corn Masa Flour

4 cups masa harina

1¼ to 2 cups warm water

Pinch of salt (optional)

1. In a medium bowl, combine the masa harina, salt, and ¼ cup of warm water. With clean hands, massage the flour and water together well until it forms a smooth and thick dough. If the dough is too sticky, sprinkle in a bit more masa harina. If the dough is too grainy, add a tablespoon of warm water at a time until it has the consistency of stiff cookie dough.

2. Form 16 golf ball–size balls, and cover them with a damp dish towel to prevent them from drying out. Continue to follow the previous cooking instructions for forming and cooking tortillas.

MAKING TORTILLAS
WITHOUT A TORTILLA PRESS

On a clean work surface, place one sheet of prepared plastic or parchment, add the masa ball to the center, and then top with the second sheet of plastic or parchment. In place of a tortilla press, use a heavy baking dish or pan to shape the tortilla to the appropriate thickness.

Green Tortillas

½ pound spinach leaves, rinsed

4 cups masa harina

Kosher salt

1. Fill a large pot with water, and add a few generous pinches of salt. Bring to a rolling boil over high heat; then add the spinach and cook for 30 seconds, until the leaves become a brighter green color. Drain the spinach. Transfer the drained spinach to a blender, add 3 cups of water, and purée on high speed until very smooth. Strain the spinach juice through a fine-mesh strainer into a large mixing bowl and add the masa harina. With clean hands, massage together the masa and spinach juice, and follow the instructions for making tortillas using masa harina.

Red Tortillas

5 large beets, peeled and diced

4 cups masa harina

Kosher salt

1. Add the beets to a juicer, and juice. In a large mixing bowl, add the beet juice to the masa harina and a pinch of salt; then add only enough water to achieve a stiff cookie dough consistency. For example, if you have 2 cups of beet juice and 4 cups of masa harina, you will likely need at least 1 to 1½ cups of water. With clean hands, massage together the masa and beet juice, and then follow the instructions for making tortillas using masa harina.

REHEATING TORTILLAS

Warming tortillas before using them is important, to ensure that they are aromatic, bend easily, and do not fall apart when you eat them. Of the many ways to reheat a tortilla, the most common method is to drizzle a little vegetable oil into a hot pan and warm the tortilla on each side for 30 to 45 seconds, then wrap it in a clean dish towel to steam for a few minutes.

Roasted Squash Flautas with Red Chile Crema and Salsa Verde

Difficulty: Medium
Prep Time: 30 minutes
Cook Time: 1 hour
Yield: 4 to 6 servings
Dietary Notes: Vegetarian, Gluten Free

Giant squashes flood the market's shelves every year around the fall holidays. Many families such as the Riveras like to leave out some of these gorgeous gourds so their ancestors can enjoy them before returning to the Land of the Dead. These easy-to-love flautas feature a hearty vegetarian filling using winter squash that is perfectly balanced with a spicy crema and a bright salsa.

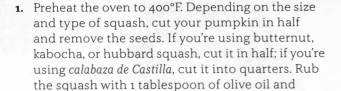

4 pounds pumpkin squash, such as butternut, kabocha, hubbard, or calabaza de Castilla

2 tablespoons olive oil, divided

Kosher salt

Black pepper

1 white onion, diced

2 garlic cloves, minced

1 cup cilantro, chopped

12 corn tortillas, homemade (page 26) or good-quality store bought, warmed

1 cup vegetable oil, for frying

1 cup queso fresco, crumbled

Salsa Verde (page 74), for garnish

RED CHILE CREMA

¾ cup Mexican crema or sour cream

¼ cup mayonnaise

½ lemon, juiced (about 1½ to 2 tablespoons)

1 tablespoon ground ancho or guajillo chile

1 garlic clove, microplaned

1 teaspoon kosher salt

¼ teaspoon freshly ground black pepper

1. Preheat the oven to 400°F. Depending on the size and type of squash, cut your pumpkin in half and remove the seeds. If you're using butternut, kabocha, or hubbard squash, cut it in half; if you're using *calabaza de Castilla*, cut it into quarters. Rub the squash with 1 tablespoon of olive oil and generously sprinkle with salt and pepper.

2. Line a baking sheet with parchment paper or a silicone mat, and place pumpkin pieces on the sheet, cut side down. Bake for 30 to 45 minutes, until the flesh of the pumpkin is easily pierced with the tip of a knife. When finished, remove the pieces from the oven and let them cool.

3. Warm the remaining 1 tablespoon of oil in a saucepan over medium heat; then add the onion, garlic, and a pinch of salt. Cook until the onions are translucent; then remove them from the heat while you make the crema and finish preparing the pumpkin.

Continued on page 32

Continued from page 31

TO MAKE THE RED CHILE CREMA:

1. Mix together the crema, mayonnaise, lemon juice, ground ancho, garlic, salt, and pepper in a small bowl; taste and adjust the salt, as needed. Set aside while you prepare the filling for the flautas.

2. Using a spoon, scrape the flesh of the pumpkin away from the peel and place it in a large mixing bowl. Roughly mash the pumpkin; then mix in the sautéed onions and chopped cilantro. Taste and adjust the salt, as needed.

3. To assemble the flautas, place a warmed tortilla in your hand and add 2 to 3 tablespoons of pumpkin filling; then roll up the tortilla tightly.

To keep the flautas from opening up while frying, insert a toothpick through 2 to 3 flautas to keep them together.

4. Warm the vegetable oil in a medium sauté pan (see first bullet in Fry Station and Safety below) over medium-high heat. Place half the flautas in the oil and cook until the tortillas are golden brown, 3 to 5 minutes. Remove the flautas from the oil and transfer them to a wire rack to cool; sprinkle them with salt while the flautas are still warm. Continue cooking the remaining flautas.

5. To serve, portion flautas on plates; then garnish with the Red Chile Crema, Salsa Verde, and crumbled queso fresco.

Fry Station and Safety

KEEP IN MIND SOME IMPORTANT
SAFETY TIPS WHEN DEEP FRYING:

- If you don't have a dedicated deep fryer, use a Dutch oven or a high-walled sauté pan.

- Never put too much oil in the pan! You don't want hot oil spilling out as soon as you put the food in.

- Use a cooking oil with a high smoke point, such as canola, peanut, or vegetable oil.

- Keep track of the oil temperature with a thermometer. The oil should be around 350°F.

- Avoid overcrowding a pan with too much food at the same time.

- Add only dry foods to your pan. Wet ingredients will splatter and can cause burns.

- Always have a lid nearby to cover the pan, in case it starts to spill over or catch fire. A properly rated fire extinguisher is also great to have on hand, in case of emergencies.

- Don't leave the pan unattended, and never let children near the pan.

- Never, ever put your face, your hand, or any other body part near the hot oil.

Grilled Fish Tacos with Cilantro-Lime Crema & Cabbage Salad

Difficulty: Medium
Prep Time: 10 minutes
Cook Time: 30 minutes
Yield: 4 to 5 servings
Dietary Notes: Gluten Free

Underground river caves, or *cenotes,* are common in parts of Mexico and can be truly miraculous natural wonders. As Miguel and Héctor find out, though, they're not great places to be imprisoned by Ernesto de la Cruz. Mama Imelda's spirit guide rescues them just in time to save the family. If they were down there much longer, they'd need to find fish in the cenote and get creative to eat, maybe with this taco recipe.

CABBAGE SALAD

Juice of 6 to 8 limes (about ½ cup)

1 tablespoon dried Mexican oregano

1½ teaspoons kosher salt

¼ cup extra virgin olive oil

¼ small green cabbage, sliced very thinly (about 4 cups)

1 carrot, peeled and shaved with a vegetable peeler

CILANTRO-LIME CREMA

½ cup Mexican crema

⅓ cup mayonnaise

¼ cup cilantro, chopped

1 lime, zest and juice

1 garlic clove, microplaned

½ teaspoon kosher salt

FISH

Vegetable oil, to grease the grill

1 pound skinless snapper, cod, or halibut filets

1 teaspoon ground coriander

1½ teaspoons smoked paprika

1 teaspoon kosher salt

½ teaspoon freshly ground black pepper

½ teaspoon cayenne

2 tablespoons extra virgin olive oil

12 corn tortillas, homemade (page 26) or good-quality store bought, warmed

Salsa Roja (page 43) or Pico de Gallo (page 35)

2 limes, cut into wedges

TO MAKE THE CABBAGE SALAD:

1. Combine the lime juice, oregano, and salt in a medium mixing bowl and whisk until the salt is dissolved. Whisk in the oil, add the cabbage and carrot, and toss to coat evenly. Set aside.

TO MAKE THE CILANTRO-LIME CREMA:

2. Combine the crema, mayonnaise, cilantro, lime zest and juice, garlic, and salt in a small bowl, and mix together. Taste and adjust salt as needed. If the crema is too thick, add a bit more lime juice or crema to thin it out. If it is too thin, add a little more mayonnaise and set it aside.

TO MAKE THE FISH:

3. Grease the grates of an outdoor grill or grill pan with vegetable oil, and then heat over medium-high heat. Rinse the fish and pat it completely dry.

In a small bowl, mix the coriander, paprika, salt, pepper, and cayenne; then sprinkle the seasonings evenly over both sides of the fish.

4. When the grill is hot and just barely smoking, drizzle olive oil over the fish and then place it on the grill. Cook the fish until it appears charred and opaque, about 4 minutes for each side of the filet. Remove the fish from the grill to a clean pan; then cut or flake the fish into smaller pieces for making tacos.

5. To serve, place the grilled fish on a warm tortilla and garnish with the crema and salsa of your choice, cabbage salad, and a lime wedge for squeezing.

USING AN OVEN

After seasoning and rubbing oil on the fish filet, you can also bake it in an oven preheated to 350°F for 10 to 12 minutes.

Grilled Steak Tacos with Chorizo Pinto Beans

Difficulty: Medium
Prep Time: 10 minutes (plus at least 1 hour wait time)
Cook Time: 20 minutes
Yield: 4 to 6 servings
Dietary Notes: Dairy Free, Gluten Free

On weekends, many families head outdoors to gather and cook their meals. In this recipe, tender steaks and meaty beans are paired with tangy pickled onions and a fresh salsa. Combined, the flavors make any cookout feel like a special occasion.

4 large limes (about ½ cup juice)

1 teaspoon kosher salt

½ teaspoon freshly ground black pepper

1 teaspoon dried Mexican oregano

½ cup vegetable oil

2 pounds skirt steak, tenderized with a meat mallet

10 to 12 corn tortillas, homemade (page 26) or good-quality store bought, warmed

Cebollas Encurtidas (page 89), for garnish

Chopped cilantro, for garnish

Lime wedges, for garnish

CHORIZO PINTO BEANS

1 tablespoon vegetable oil

½ white onion, diced

2 garlic cloves, minced

½ teaspoon ground cumin

¼ teaspoon ground chipotle powder

4 ounces Mexican chorizo, casings removed

4 cups of pinto beans plus ¼ cup bean broth, using the Frijoles de la Olla recipe (page 82)

Salt

Black pepper

PICO DE GALLO

½ small red onion, finely diced

2 limes, juiced

Kosher salt

3 Roma tomatoes, finely diced

¼ packed cup cilantro, chopped

1 serrano chile, seeded and finely diced (optional)

½ bunch scallions, thinly sliced

TO MAKE THE GRILLED STEAK

1. Zest 2 of the limes into a large bowl or baking dish; then juice all 4 limes into the bowl. Add the salt, pepper, oregano, and ½ cup of oil, and whisk together. Place the meat in the lime marinade, and refrigerate for at least 1 hour and up to 4 hours. If making just the steak, skip to step 4

TO MAKE THE CHORIZO PINTO BEANS:

2. In a medium sauté pan, heat the oil over medium heat until the oil just starts to simmer. Add the onion and sauté until softened. Add the garlic, cumin, and chipotle; stir to combine and bloom the dried spices, 1 minute. Add the chorizo and cook, breaking up the meat with a spoon or wooden spatula until the fat is mostly rendered and the meat is browned, about 5 minutes. Add the beans, bean broth, and 2 tablespoons of water; simmer until thickened, about 5 minutes. Season the beans with salt and black pepper, as needed. Cover the beans, and keep them warm over low heat.

TO MAKE THE PICO DE GALLO:

3. In a medium mixing bowl, combine onion, lime juice, and a generous pinch of salt. Stir everything together and let it sit for 10 minutes, to mellow the sharp flavor of the raw onion. Add the tomatoes, cilantro, serrano, and scallions, and combine. Taste and adjust the seasoning, as needed.

4. To cook the steak, preheat an outdoor grill or grill pan over high heat. Remove the steak from the marinade and add it to the grill; let it cook for about 3 minutes on each side. Remove the steak from the grill and let it rest for 5 minutes. Slice the steak against the grain into ¼-inch thick strips.

5. To assemble, divide the steak among the tortillas. Garnish the tacos with the Chorizo Pinto Beans, Pico de Gallo, *Cebollas Encurtidas*, chopped cilantro, and lime wedges.

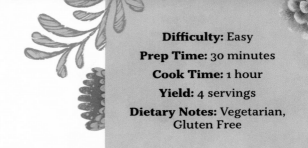

Quesadillas con Hongos

Quesadillas with Sautéed Mushrooms

Difficulty: Easy
Prep Time: 30 minutes
Cook Time: 1 hour
Yield: 4 servings
Dietary Notes: Vegetarian, Gluten Free

Mexican street food is globally recognized and loved for its complex and explosive flavors. Inspired by the many street food vendors on both sides of the Marigold Bridge, this recipe amps up the flavor of the already-irresistible quesadilla with earthy sautéed mushrooms, creamy avocado salsa, and tangy pickled onions.

AVOCADO SALSA

½ pound tomatillos, cleaned, husked and stemmed

½ bunch of cilantro, thick stems removed

2 garlic cloves, peeled

2 avocados, halved, pitted, and peeled

Juice of 1 lime

½ to 1 serrano chile, stemmed (optional)

½ cup water, plus more as needed

½ teaspoon kosher salt

QUESADILLAS

3 tablespoons vegetable oil

½ white onion, diced

2 garlic cloves, minced

1 serrano chile, seeded and minced (optional)

1 pound white or cremini mushrooms, cleaned and sliced

¼ teaspoon kosher salt

¼ cup fresh epazote, chopped (can substitute with cilantro)

12 to 16 corn tortillas, homemade (page 26) or good-quality store bought, warmed

8 ounces queso Oaxaca (quesillo), Monterey Jack, or low-moisture mozzarella, shredded and divided

Cebollas Encurtidas (page 89)

TO MAKE THE AVOCADO SALSA:

1. Add the tomatillos, cilantro, garlic, avocados, lime juice, serrano chile, water, and salt to a food processor, and blend until smooth. Set aside.

TO MAKE THE QUESADILLAS:

2. Warm the oil in a large pan over medium-high heat. Add the onion to the pan, and sauté until translucent, about 5 minutes. Add the garlic and serrano, and stir to combine for about 1 minute.

3. Increase the heat to high. Add the sliced mushrooms, sautéing until they become dark golden brown and have released all their water, 6 to 7 minutes. Stir in the salt and epazote, and transfer to a plate for assembling the quesadillas.

4. Wipe the pan with a paper towel and set it back on the burner over medium heat. Working in batches, add the tortillas to the pan and warm them on both sides until they soften.

5. To assemble the quesadillas, add a couple tablespoons of shredded cheese and a couple tablespoons of mushrooms to a warmed tortilla; then fold over the tortilla and return it to the heated pan. Cook on each side for about 1 minute, pressing down with a heatproof spatula until the cheese is melted and the tortillas are freckled and crispy.

6. Serve immediately with the Avocado Salsa and Cebollas Encurtidas.

Enchiladas Mineras

Miner's Enchiladas

Difficulty: Medium
Prep Time: 20 minutes
Cook Time: 50 minutes
Yield: 12 enchiladas
Dietary Notes: Vegetarian, Gluten Free

One of the historic places that inspired the design of the Land of the Living can be found in the Mexican city of Guanajuato, where brightly painted homes decorate its rolling hills. These delectable enchiladas—which are dipped in chile sauce, filled with cheese, and garnished with hearty stewed vegetables—come from this area and are a hearty vegetarian meal you'll want to make over and over again.

1½ cups chicken or vegetable stock

8 guajillo chiles, stemmed and seeded

2 garlic cloves, peeled

1 teaspoon dried Mexican oregano

½ teaspoon kosher salt

¼ teaspoon freshly ground black pepper

4 tablespoons vegetable oil, divided

½ white onion, diced

1 pound red or Yukon Gold potatoes, peeled and diced small

3 medium carrots, peeled and diced small

2 tablespoons apple cider vinegar

12 corn tortillas, homemade (page 26) or good-quality store bought, warmed

2 cups queso fresco, crumbled and divided

4 red radishes, rinsed and finely diced

4 romaine lettuce leaves, rinsed and thinly sliced

¼ cup Mexican crema

Chiles en Escabeche (page 87), chopped

1. In a medium pot, bring the stock, chiles, garlic, oregano, salt, and pepper to a boil. Remove the pan from the heat, cover with a lid, and let sit for 20 minutes, until the chiles are softened. Transfer everything to a blender, and purée until very smooth.

2. In a pot over medium-high heat, add 2 tablespoons of the vegetable oil. Add the diced onion, potato, and carrot, and sauté for about 5 minutes, tossing the vegetables occasionally to cook evenly.

3. Pour the chile purée into the pot with the sautéed vegetables, and stir to incorporate, scraping off any browned bits from the bottom. Cover the pot, reduce the heat to low, and simmer until the vegetables are completely cooked but not falling apart, about 25 minutes.

4. Stir in the vinegar, cover the pan, and keep warm over low heat while you prepare the enchiladas.

5. Brush both sides of the tortillas with the remaining 2 tablespoons of vegetable oil. Heat a large skillet over medium-high heat; then, working in batches, cook the tortillas on each side for 15 to 20 seconds, until they just start to toast.

6. Using a pair of tongs, remove the tortillas from the pan and dip both sides in the vegetable-chile liquid. Place the sauced tortilla on a plate, fill it with 2 to 3 tablespoons of crumbled queso fresco, and fold the tortilla into a half-moon shape. Repeat this step until you've used all the tortillas.

7. To serve, use a slotted spoon to remove the potatoes, carrots, and onion from the sauce, and add them to the top of the filled enchiladas. Add diced radish and sliced romaine lettuce, and garnish with crema and chopped *Chiles en Escabeche*.

Enchiladas Suizas

Baked Swiss Enchiladas

Difficulty: Easy
Prep Time: 20 minutes
Cook Time: 30 minutes
Yield: 6 servings
Dietary Notes: Gluten Free

The restaurant scene in Mexico City is globally renowned for its creativity, variety, and influences. One of the most popular chains of cafeteria-style restaurants in the city is rumored to have created delicious creamy, baked enchiladas that are now served throughout the country and abroad, while others claim the dish dates back to Emperor Maximilian. One thing is certain, however: These are not a real Swiss culinary invention, but that hasn't stopped millions of people from enjoying them! Try this flavorful version and see for yourself.

2 pounds tomatillos, husked and rinsed

2 small serrano chiles, stemmed

1 small white onion, quartered

4 garlic cloves, unpeeled

¼ cup chopped cilantro, plus more for garnish

2 cups store-bought chicken stock, divided

Kosher salt

Freshly ground black pepper

4 tablespoons vegetable oil, divided

½ cup Mexican crema

12 corn tortillas, homemade (page 26) or good-quality sore bought, warmed

2 poached skinless, boneless chicken breasts (prepared according to Pollo en Mole Rojo, page 66)

8 ounces shredded queso Oaxaca (quesillo), Monterey Jack, or other white melty cheese

1. Warm an ungreased pan over medium heat. When it's hot, char the tomatillos, chiles, onion, and unpeeled garlic on all sides; remove the ingredients when they are evenly blackened on all sides, about 3 minutes for the garlic and 8 to 10 minutes for the tomatillos, chiles, and onion. Alternatively, you can line a small baking sheet with aluminum foil and place the ingredients on the baking sheet; then place in a broiler to char, about 8 minutes, turning halfway to blacken evenly.

2. When the garlic is cooled slightly, peel the garlic and add all the charred ingredients to a blender, along with the cilantro, 1 cup of chicken stock, and a generous pinch of salt and pepper. Blend on high until very smooth.

3. Warm the same pan over medium-high heat; then add 2 tablespoons of oil. Pour in the puréed sauce all at once and cook, stirring constantly, until it is thickened, about 8 to 10 minutes.

4. Stir in the remaining 1 cup of stock and crema, and then simmer for a few minutes to meld the flavors. The sauce should have the consistency

of a creamy soup. Taste and add more salt, as needed. When the sauce has finished cooking, turn the heat to very low, cover, and keep warm while you fill the tortillas.

5. Preheat the oven to 400°F.

6. Heat the remaining 2 tablespoons of oil in another pan over medium heat. When hot, quickly fry the tortillas on both sides in the hot oil until they are soft and pliable, about 20 seconds per side. Transfer fried tortillas to a paper towel–lined plate to soak up excess oil.

7. Smear approximately 1 cup of sauce over the bottom of a 9-by-13-inch baking dish. Stuff each tortilla with 2 to 3 tablespoons of shredded chicken, roll up the tortillas tightly, and place them seam side down in the baking dish in a single layer. Pour the remaining sauce over the top of the stuffed tortillas, sprinkle with the shredded cheese, and then bake until the cheese starts to brown, 15 to 20 minutes.

8. Serve immediately, garnished with more chopped cilantro.

Difficulty: Easy
Prep Time: 20 minutes
Cook Time: 30 minutes
Yield: 4 servings
Dietary Notes: Vegetarian, Dairy Free

Chilaquiles

If there are leftover tortillas from a big fiesta, everyone looks forward to this dish for breakfast the next day. *Chilaquiles* are a humble dish with anything-but-simple flavors. A perfect way to use older tortillas and bits and pieces from other recipes, chilaquiles are a reminder of the great times that were had.

10 corn tortillas, homemade (page 26) or good-quality store bought, preferably a day old

1 cup vegetable oil

Kosher salt

2 cups Salsa Verde (page 74) or Salsa Roja (page 43)

OPTIONAL GARNISHES

Fried or scrambled eggs

Shredded chicken (page 67)

Pasta de Frijol (page 86)

Grilled Steak (page 35), sliced

Mexican crema

Cilantro or parsley, chopped

White onion, diced

Queso fresco, crumbled

1. Leave the tortillas, uncovered, on a counter to dry out overnight.

2. Slice the tortillas into eighths, and warm the oil in a large skillet over medium-high heat. Working in batches, fry the tortilla pieces in the oil until golden brown, about 3 minutes.

3. Remove the fried tortillas from the pan with a slotted spoon, and place them on a paper towel–lined plate to soak up excess oil. Sprinkle salt over the fried tortillas while they're still hot.

4. In another large skillet over medium heat, add the salsa and bring it to a simmer. Add the fried tortillas, and mix until the chips are totally covered.

5. Serve immediately with garnishes of your choice.

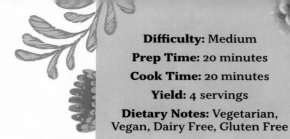

Huaraches

Black Bean-Filled Masa Cakes

Difficulty: Medium
Prep Time: 20 minutes
Cook Time: 20 minutes
Yield: 4 servings
Dietary Notes: Vegetarian, Vegan, Dairy Free, Gluten Free

These filled and griddled masa cakes get their name from the oval-shape sole of a Mexican sandal. As a family of shoemakers, the Riveras can certainly appreciate this dish. Miguel isn't as thrilled as everyone else to join the family business (he's meant to be a musician!), but even he could love these "shoes."

1 pound fresh masa or 1¾ cups masa harina mixed with about 1½ cups warm water

1 cup Pasta de Frijol with black beans (page 86)

½ cup white onion, diced

3 to 4 red radishes, sliced thinly

½ cup cilantro, chopped

Avocado Salsa (page 36) and/or Salsa Roja (page 43)

Mexican crema (optional)

Queso fresco, crumbled (optional)

2 limes, cut into wedges

1. Preheat a large ungreased saucepan over medium heat.

2. If using masa harina, knead 1½ cups of warm water into the masa until it forms a dense dough. With the hydrated masa harina or fresh masa, form one ½-cup size ball of masa into an egg shape. Using your thumb, make a deep, wide indentation; fill it with a spoonful of the *Pasta de Frijol*. Pinch the masa together to enclose the beans, and then roll it into a cigar shape.

3. Place one sheet of plastic on a clean work surface; put the masa in the middle, and cover with the second sheet of plastic. Use a rolling pin to roll out the *huarache* into a long oval shape, about 8 inches long and ¼ inch thick.

4. Carefully peel off the top sheet of plastic, flip the masa onto your fingers, and peel off the bottom sheet of plastic.

5. After removing the plastic from the prepared huarache, transfer it quickly to the warm pan, and cook on one side for 1 to 2 minutes. Flip over the huarache and cook for a few more minutes on the other side. The masa should be slightly crisp and freckled. Repeat steps 2 through 5 with the remaining masa. Wrap finished huaraches in a clean dish towel to keep them warm.

6. To serve, garnish huaraches with onion, radishes, cilantro, salsas, crema, and queso (if using), as well as lime wedges for squeezing.

Salsa Roja
Red Salsa

6 Roma tomatoes, halved lengthwise

2 serrano chiles, stemmed and deseeded

2 jalapeño chiles, stemmed and deseeded

¼ white onion, halved

3 garlic cloves, peeled

12 cilantro stalks

Kosher salt

1. In a medium-sized pot, add the tomatoes, serrano and jalapeño chiles, onion, and garlic, and cover the ingredients with 2 cups of water. Bring the water to a boil over high heat then reduce the heat to a simmer and cook for 15 minutes, until the tomatoes start to break apart and chiles turn to a darker green color.

2. Add the mixture to a blender, along with the cilantro and 2 teaspoons of salt to start. Puree the ingredients on high until smooth, about 30 seconds, then taste and adjust seasonings as needed. Salsa is best enjoyed after a few hours so the flavors infuse more. Transfer to an airtight container and store in the refrigerator for up to 5 days.

Tamales Salados

Savory Tamales

Tamales have many shapes, sizes, and flavors. They can be small and round without any fillings, or they can be wrapped in banana leaves and several feet long, or anything in between. The most important part of making any tamal is correctly preparing the masa. To save time and energy, this recipe uses a stand mixer for whipping up fluffy masa.

24 large corn husks, plus more to cover the steamer

6 cups fresh masa or 4 cups masa harina for tamales

1 teaspoon baking powder

1 tablespoon kosher salt

2 cups lard (or softened unsalted butter or vegetable shortening)

¼ cup to 3 cups room-temperature meat or vegetable stock

SUGGESTED FILLINGS

Rajas con Queso (Roasted Poblano Strips and Cheese, page 46)

Frijoles con Queso (Beans and Cheese, page 46)

Pollo en Mole Rojo (Chicken in Red Mole, page 66)

Pollo en Salsa Verde (Chicken in Green Salsa, page 47)

Picadillo (Spiced Ground Beef, page 63)

1. While preparing the tamal dough, soak the corn husks in very hot water until softened, about 30 minutes. Weight down the husks with a heavy dish or mugs, to keep them submerged.

2. If using masa harina, add the masa harina, baking powder, and salt to the bowl of a stand mixer; whisk together. Add the lard, and then beat the mixture over medium speed with the paddle attachment to combine. Gradually add 3 cups of stock, and continue beating on low speed until incorporated.

3. If using fresh masa, moisten the dough with ¼ cup of stock and beat on low speed until incorporated. Add the baking powder, salt, and lard, and beat on medium speed. Whip the dough until it is very fluffy.

TIP:

To test if the dough is sufficiently whipped, drop a small piece of masa into a glass of water: If it floats, it is ready. If the dough sinks, add more fat by the tablespoon and continue whipping on medium-high speed. The dough should spread easily like a thick muffin batter or hummus.

Difficulty: Medium
Prep Time: 1 hour
(plus 30 minutes wait time)
Cook Time: 1½ hours
Yield: 24 tamales
Dietary Notes: Dairy Free,
Gluten Free

4. To assemble, remove the corn husks from the water and lay them out on a clean work surface, with the smoother side of the husk facing up. If the husk is small, double up with another small husk. If a husk has any holes, discard it and wrap with another husk.

5. Working one at a time, place ¼ cup of the prepared masa in the center of the corn husk. Then evenly spread out the masa to about ¼-inch thickness using a spoon, offset spatula, or silicone spatula, leaving a 1½-inch border on the sides of the husk.

6. Add the filling of your choice, then fold in the sides of the husk to cover it. Fold over the narrow, pointy end of the husk to form a packet, leaving the opposite end of the husk open.

7. In a steamer, add enough water to reach just under the bottom of the steamer insert. If there are any unused corn husks, layer them on top of the steamer insert. Set the filled tamales in a steamer basket on top of the husks, stacking them vertically, with the open ends of the tamales facing up. When all the tamales are filled and packed tightly in the steamer, cover the top of the tamales with extra husks before putting the lid on.

8. Steam the tamales on medium to medium-high heat for 1 to 1½ hours. To test doneness, carefully remove a tamal from the pot and set aside to cool for 5 minutes before peeling back the husk. The masa should be firm and pull away cleanly from the husk.

9. Let the tamales cool for about 10 minutes before serving.

STORING & REHEATING TAMALES

Cooked tamales can be stored in the refrigerator in an airtight container for up to 5 days. If frozen, they can last up to 6 months. To reheat, thaw the wrapped tamales in the refrigerator overnight and steam them for 10 minutes before serving.

Vegetarian Fillings for Tamales

To keep the entire dish vegetarian, use butter or vegetable shortening instead of lard. Be sure to separate these tamales from any nonvegetarian tamales in the pot so you can easily keep track of them. All filling recipe amounts work best with 1 recipe of the dough made in Tamales Salados (page 44).

Rajas con Queso

Roasted Poblano Strips and Cheese

8 large poblano chiles or 2 cups canned whole roasted poblano chiles

1 pound queso Oaxaca (quesillo), Monterey Jack, or other white melty cheese, cut into 3-by-½-inch strips

2 cups Salsa Verde (page 74)

1. For fresh whole chiles, turn one burner of a gas burner or outdoor grill to medium-high heat. With tongs, place poblano chiles directly over the flame and char until blackened on all sides. Alternatively, you can place chiles on a foil-lined baking pan under the broiler for 10 to 15 minutes, turning halfway to char evenly. Transfer cooked chiles to a large heatproof bowl, and cover with plastic wrap or a clean kitchen towel to steam for 15 to 20 minutes.

2. Transfer the chiles to a cutting board and, by hand or with the back of a knife, carefully remove the blistered skins, seeds, and stems. Slice the chiles into thin strips, and set them aside.

3. If using canned whole chiles, simply drain and slice the chiles into thin strips.

4. To assemble the tamales, place a few strips of roasted chiles and cheese in the center of the dough. Follow the instructions for cooking tamales. Garnish with Salsa Verde when ready to serve.

Frijoles con Queso

Beans and Cheese

4 cups Pasta de Frijol with black beans (page 86)

1 pound queso Oaxaca (quesillo), Monterey Jack, or other white melty cheese, cut into Like 3-by-½-inch strips

Salsa of your choice

1. Add about 2 tablespoons of Pasta de Frijol to each tamal, along with a couple strips of cheese. Follow the provided instructions for cooking tamales. Garnish with your preferred salsa when ready to serve.

Meat Fillings For Tamales

Many factors go into making great tamales, including the type of masa and fat you use. When it comes to fillings, it's easiest to use precooked ingredients that are cooled completely. This helps with portioning and prevents the fat in the masa from melting while assembling. All filling recipe amounts work best with 1 recipe of the dough made in Tamales Salados (page 44).

Pollo en Mole Rojo

Chicken in Red Mole

5 cups Pollo en Mole Rojo (page 66)

1. Shred or cut the chicken, and mix it back into the *mole rojo*. Portion 3 tablespoons of prepared *Pollo en Mole Rojo* to each tamal; then follow the instructions for cooking tamales.

Pollo en Salsa Verde

Chicken in Green Salsa

3 to 4 skinless, boneless chicken breasts (prepared according to instructions in Pollo en Mole Rojo on page 67), shredded

4 cups Salsa Verde (page 74), prepared with an additional 2 cups water when cooking

1. Place 2 to 3 tablespoons of shredded chicken in each tamal, and top with 2 to 3 tablespoons of Salsa Verde. Follow the instructions for cooking tamales.

Picadillo

Spiced Ground Beef

5 cups Picadillo (page 63)

1. Portion 3 tablespoons of prepared Picadillo to each tamal; then follow the instructions for cooking tamales.

Tamales Dulces

Dessert Tamales

Tamal de Chocolate

Chocolate Tamal

Difficulty: Medium
Prep Time: 1 hour
(plus 30 minutes wait time)
Cook Time: 1½ hours
Yield: 24 tamales
Dietary Notes: Vegetarian,
Gluten Free

Just when everyone thinks the tamal feast is over, Abuelita is likely to offer the family *Tamales Dulces* (dessert tamales)—and she doesn't take, *"No, gracias,"* for an answer. The process and technique for making sweet tamales are similar to those for savory tamales, but a few changes are needed to make them perfect as a sweet treat. Dessert tamal options abound, but the chocolate and strawberry recipes here are surely two of the most vibrantly colored.

24 large corn husks, plus more to cover the steamer

4 cups fresh masa or 4 cups masa harina for tamales

¼ cup unsweetened cocoa powder

½ teaspoon baking powder

¼ teaspoon kosher salt

⅔ cup sugar

1 cup butter, softened

1 cup whole milk or unsweetened plant-based milk

1 teaspoon vanilla extract

2 cups (one 12-ounce bag) bittersweet chocolate chips, coarsely chopped (optional)

1. While preparing the tamal dough, soak the corn husks in very hot water until softened, about 30 minutes. Weight down the husks with a heavy dish or mugs, to keep them submerged.

2. If using masa harina, combine the flour with the cocoa powder, baking powder, and salt in a large bowl. Add enough water until it feels like a dense cookie dough, about 3 to 3½ cups water. If using fresh masa, combine the cocoa powder, baking powder, and salt with the ⅔ cup sugar in a separate small bowl, and set aside.

3. In the bowl of a stand mixer with a paddle attachment, add the masa and whip on medium-high speed until very fluffy. The more the masa is whipped, the lighter the tamales will be when cooked.

4. After beating for a few minutes, add the softened butter 1 to 2 tablespoons at a time until incorporated. Then add the sugar (or sugar and cocoa mixture) and mix for another couple minutes.

5. Add the milk and vanilla extract to the mixing bowl, and continue beating on medium speed. At this stage, the masa should spread easily like a thick muffin batter or hummus.

6. To assemble, remove the corn husks from the water and lay them out on a clean work surface, with the smooth side of the husk facing up. If the husk is small, double

up with another smaller husk; similarly, if the husk has any holes, wrap it with another husk.

7. Working one at a time, place a heaping ¼ to ⅓ cup of masa in the center of the corn husk, depending on the size of the husk. Then evenly spread out the masa to about ¼-inch thickness using a spoon, offset spatula, or silicone spatula, leaving a 1½-inch border on the sides of the husk. Sprinkle chopped chocolate down the center of the masa; then fold the sides of the husk to cover it. Fold over the narrow, pointy end of the husk to form a packet, leaving the opposite end of the husk open.

8. In a steamer, add enough water to reach just under the bottom of the steamer insert. If there are any unused corn husks, layer them on top of the steamer insert. Set the filled tamales in the steamer basket on top of the husks, stacking them vertically with the open ends of the tamales facing up. When all the tamales are filled and packed tightly in the steamer, cover the top of the tamales with extra husks before putting the lid on.

9. Steam the tamales on medium to medium-high heat for 1 to 1½ hours. To test doneness, carefully remove a tamal from the pot and set aside to cool for 5 minutes before peeling back the husk. The masa should be firm and pull away cleanly from the husk.

10. Let the tamales cool for about 10 minutes before serving.

Tamal de Fresa
Strawberry Tamal

Difficulty: Medium
Prep Time: 1 hour
(plus 30 minutes wait time)
Cook Time: 1½ hours
Yield: 24 tamales
Dietary Notes: Vegetarian,
Gluten Free

In late summer, the *mercado* (market) overflows with the most colorful berries. Eating these little jewels by the handful is a joy, as they burst with tart-sweet juices. Using strawberries and berry jam in these tamales makes them taste like a delicate sponge cake wrapped in corn husks.

- 24 large corn husks, plus more to cover the steamer
- 2 cups strawberries, diced finely
- 1 cup milk
- 1 teaspoon vanilla extract
- 3 drops red food coloring (optional)
- 4 cups fresh masa or 4 cups masa harina for tamales
- ½ teaspoon baking powder
- ½ teaspoon kosher salt
- ½ cup sugar
- 1 cup butter, softened
- 2 cups strawberry jam

1. While preparing the tamal dough, soak the corn husks in very hot water until softened, about 30 minutes. Weight down the husks with a heavy dish or mugs, to keep them submerged.

2. In a large bowl, combine the diced strawberries with the milk, vanilla extract, and red food coloring (if using).

3. If using masa harina, combine the flour with the baking powder and salt; then add enough water until it feels like a dense cookie dough, about 3 to 3½ cups water. If using fresh masa, combine the baking powder and salt with the ½ cup sugar in a separate small bowl, and set aside.

4. In the bowl of a stand mixer with a paddle attachment, add the masa and whip on medium-high speed until very fluffy. The more the masa is whipped, the lighter the tamales will be when cooked. After beating for a few minutes, add the softened butter 1 to 2 tablespoons at a time until incorporated. Then add the sugar (or sugar and baking soda mixture) and mix for another couple minutes.

5. Add the strawberry and milk mixture, and continue beating on low speed to incorporate. At this stage, the masa should spread easily like a thick muffin batter or hummus.

6. To assemble, remove the corn husks from the water and lay them out on a clean work surface, with the smooth side of the husk facing up. If the husk is small, double up with another smaller husk; similarly, if the husk has any holes, wrap it with another husk.

7. Working one at a time, place a heaping ¼ to ⅓ cup of masa in the center of the corn husk, depending on the size of the husk. Then evenly spread out the masa to about ¼-inch thickness using a spoon, offset spatula, or silicone spatula, leaving a 1½-inch border on the sides of the husk. Add about 1 tablespoon of strawberry jam to the center of the masa, and then fold the sides of the husk to cover it. Fold over the narrow, pointy end of the husk to form a packet, leaving the opposite end of the husk open.

8. In a steamer, add enough water to reach just under the bottom of the steamer insert. If there are any unused corn husks, layer them on top of the steamer insert. Set the filled tamales in the steamer basket on top of the husks, stacking them vertically with the open ends of the tamales facing up. When all the tamales are filled and packed tightly in the steamer, cover the top of the tamales with extra husks before putting the lid on.

9. Steam the tamales on medium to medium-high heat for 1 to 1½ hours. To test doneness, carefully remove a tamal from the pot and set aside to cool for 5 minutes before peeling back the husk. The masa should be firm and pull away cleanly from the husk.

10. Let the tamales cool for about 10 minutes before serving.

Platos Fuertes

MAIN DISHES

Acelgas con Garbanzo

Stewed Swiss Chard with Chickpeas

Difficulty: Easy
Prep Time: 10 minutes
Cook Time: 25 minutes
Yield: 4 servings
Dietary Notes: Vegan, Dairy Free, Gluten Free

When Miguel skips through Santa Cecilia in the film, he passes many produce vendors selling garden-fresh ingredients. From ripe and juicy tomatoes to bouquets of leafy greens, these humble ingredients can be easily transformed into a delicious vegetarian meal.

1 pound Swiss chard (about 2 bunches), rinsed, with leaves and stems separated

3 tablespoons extra virgin olive oil

½ white onion, sliced

3 garlic cloves, thinly sliced

1 Roma tomato, chopped

1 tablespoon tomato paste

2 cups cooked garbanzo beans (or one 15½-ounce can, drained)

½ teaspoon kosher salt

½ teaspoon ground cumin

¼ teaspoon cayenne powder or another chile powder

½ cup stock or water

Lime wedges, to garnish

1. Roughly chop the chard leaves and dice the stems into ½-inch pieces. Set aside.

2. Warm the olive oil in a large sauté pan over medium-high heat. Add the onion and diced chard stems, and sauté for 5 minutes, until translucent and softened. Add the sliced garlic and cook until fragrant, 1 minute.

3. Add the chopped tomato and sauté until the pieces soften slightly. Stir in the tomato paste, add the chard leaves, and cook until the leaves start to wilt.

4. Add the cooked garbanzos, salt, cumin, cayenne powder, and stock; cook until all the liquid in the pan thickens slightly. Adjust the seasonings, as needed. Serve warm with a wedge of lime, and accompany with sides such as *Arroz Blanco* (page 83), *Frijoles de la Olla* (page 82), and warmed *Tortillas de Maíz* (page 26).

Tortitas de Papa

Potato Fritters in Tomato Sauce

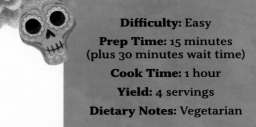

Difficulty: Easy

Prep Time: 15 minutes (plus 30 minutes wait time)

Cook Time: 1 hour

Yield: 4 servings

Dietary Notes: Vegetarian

This homey recipe uses many pantry-friendly ingredients to make a filling and satisfying meal. Abuelita could quickly whip up this type of recipe to feed the family after a long day's work in the shoemaking workshop. The potato fritters can be cooked ahead of time and reheated in the oven for 10 minutes at 350°F.

POTATO FRITTERS

2 pounds Yukon Gold potatoes

1 teaspoon kosher salt, plus more to taste

2 eggs

2 tablespoons panko breadcrumbs

½ cup queso fresco, crumbled

4 tablespoons vegetable oil

TOMATO SAUCE

1 pound Roma tomatoes

1 jalapeño chile, stemmed and seeded

¼ cup white onion, chopped

3 garlic cloves

¼ teaspoon cumin seed

1 teaspoon kosher salt

Pinch of freshly ground black pepper

1 tablespoon vegetable oil

2 to 3 tablespoons chopped fresh cilantro or parsley

TO MAKE THE POTATO FRITTERS:

1. In a large pot, add the potatoes, a very generous pinch of salt, and enough water to completely cover them. Bring the water to a boil, cover the pot, and cook for 30 to 40 minutes or until the potatoes are easily pierced with a toothpick.

2. Drain the potatoes over a colander; discard the water. Let the potatoes cool before handling; then peel off the skins and place the peeled potatoes in a large mixing bowl. Mash the potatoes with a fork or masher, add the eggs and 1 teaspoon of salt, and continue mashing until the mixture forms a dough. Mix in the breadcrumbs and crumbled queso fresco.

3. Portion ¼ cup of dough, and roll into compact balls. Flatten each ball slightly to make a disk that's about ½-inch thick. Heat 4 tablespoons of vegetable oil in a medium sauté pan over medium-high heat; add the potato disks and fry until golden brown, 4 to 5 minutes on each side. Remove the disks from the pan, and place them on a paper towel–lined plate to soak up excess oil.

TO MAKE THE TOMATO BROTH:

4. Place the tomatoes, jalapeño, onion, garlic, cumin seed, salt, pepper, and 1 cup of water in a blender, and purée until very smooth. Heat the oil in a large pan over medium-high heat; add the tomato broth, and bring to a simmer. Add the cilantro or parsley, and taste and adjust seasoning or water, as needed.

5. To serve, place a few potato fritters on a plate and ladle the tomato sauce over each fritter.

Rajas con Crema

Roasted Poblano Strips in Cream Sauce

Difficulty: Easy
Prep Time: 10 minutes (plus 20 minutes wait time)
Cook Time: 25 minutes
Yield: 4 servings
Dietary Notes: Vegetarian, Gluten Free

Even los muertos crave the homey meals they enjoyed in their hometown *fondas* (casual family eateries). Mexican-style stews, such as these charred poblano chiles simmered in a creamy and cheesy sauce, will satisfy your craving for comfort food. In a pinch, you can use canned whole poblano chiles and cut them into strips.

6 poblano chiles

2 tablespoons vegetable oil

1 white onion, chopped

3 garlic cloves, minced

1 ear yellow corn, kernels removed, or ½ cup frozen corn kernels

2 teaspoons kosher salt, plus more to taste

1 cup Mexican crema

1 cup vegetable stock or water

¼ cup grated queso Oaxaca (quesillo), Monterey Jack, or other white melty cheese

12 corn tortillas, homemade (page 26) or good-quality store bought, warmed

Lime wedges, for garnishing

1. Using a gas burner or outdoor grill, turn one burner to medium-high heat. With tongs, place poblano chiles directly over the flame and char until blackened on all sides. Alternatively, you can place chiles on a foil-lined baking pan under the broiler for 10 to 15 minutes, turning halfway to char evenly. Transfer finished chiles to a heatproof bowl, and cover with plastic wrap or a clean kitchen towel to steam for 15 to 20 minutes.

2. Transfer the chiles to a cutting board and, by hand or with the back of a knife, carefully remove the blistered skins, seeds, and stems. Slice the chiles into thin strips, and set them aside.

3. Heat the vegetable oil in a large sauté pan over medium heat. Add chopped onion, and cook until it begins to soften, about 2 minutes. Add minced garlic, stirring to incorporate; then add the chile strips, corn, and salt. Reduce the heat to medium-low and cover the pan, letting the flavors meld gently for about 5 minutes.

4. Stir in the crema and the stock or water, and cook gently for about 5 minutes, until the cream mixture is warmed through.

5. Stir in grated cheese until melted, add salt to taste, and serve immediately with corn tortillas and lime wedges.

Chiles Rellenos

Stuffed Chiles in Tomato Salsa

Difficulty: Medium
Prep Time: 25 minutes
(plus 20 minutes wait time)
Cook Time: 45 minutes
Yield: 8 chiles
Dietary Notes: Vegetarian

Stuffed chiles are quintessential in traditional Mexican cuisine, and this is one of the most classic versions. Preparing the chiles and then filling and frying them takes some time, but you're certain to go *un poquito loco* in the best way when you enjoy the finished dish.

TOMATO SALSA

4 Roma tomatoes, cored and quartered

1 small white onion, peeled and quartered

3 garlic cloves,

1 tablespoon tomato paste

1 tablespoon salt

1 cup water or stock

1 teaspoon dried Mexican oregano

2 tablespoons vegetable oil

CHILES

8 medium poblano chiles

4 cups queso Oaxaca (quesillo), Monterey Jack, or other white melty cheese, shredded and divided

4 medium eggs, whites and yolks separated

¼ teaspoon cream of tartar

2½ teaspoons kosher salt, divided

1 teaspoon freshly ground black pepper, divided

1 cup all-purpose flour

2 cups vegetable oil, plus more as needed

TO MAKE THE TOMATO SALSA:

1. Add the tomatoes, onion, garlic, tomato paste, salt, water or stock, and oregano to a blender, and purée until very smooth. Heat the oil in a large sauté pan over medium heat, add the sauce, and simmer for 30 minutes, stirring occasionally, until slightly thickened but easily pourable. Set aside.

TO MAKE THE CHILES:

2. Using a gas burner or outdoor grill, turn one burner to medium-high heat. With tongs, place poblano chiles directly over the flame and char until blackened on all sides. Alternatively, you can place chiles on a foil-lined baking pan under the broiler for 10 to 15 minutes, turning halfway to char evenly. Transfer finished chiles to a heatproof bowl, and cover with plastic wrap or a clean kitchen towel to steam for 15 to 20 minutes.

3. Remove chiles from the bowl, and gently scrape off the charred skin from the chile with your hands or the back of a knife. Carefully, make a lengthwise cut down the side of the chile, leaving 1 inch from the stem and the tip of the chile. It is important not to completely cut open the chile, or it will fall apart when filled. Gently remove and discard seeds.

4. Fill each chile with roughly ½ cup of cheese, and seal the chile by threading a toothpick through the opening.

5. Place the egg whites, cream of tartar, 2 teaspoons salt, and ½ teaspoon black pepper in the bowl of a stand mixer with a whisk attachment, and beat until the mixture reaches stiff peaks, about 5 minutes. Add the egg yolks and mix gently; be careful not to overmix the egg whites, or they will lose their volume.

6. Prepare a separate plate with the flour and remaining salt and pepper. Heat the vegetable oil in a large sauté pan over medium heat.

7. Holding the stem of the chile, roll the chile in the flour mixture and then in the batter until it is completely covered.

8. Carefully place the chile in the pan, and fry for about 1 minute on each side until the chile is golden brown. Remove it from the oil when finished, and place on a paper towel-lined plate to absorb excess oil. Repeat with the remaining chiles.

9. To serve, spoon a generous amount of the salsa onto a plate or a serving platter. Remove the toothpick from each chile, and place the chiles on top of the salsa, spooning more salsa over the fried chiles.

Photograph features Salsa Verde, rather than the Tomato Salsa from this recipe.

Camarones a la Diabla

Deviled Shrimp

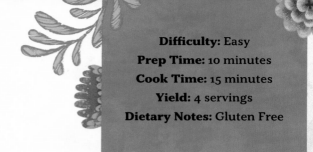

Difficulty: Easy
Prep Time: 10 minutes
Cook Time: 15 minutes
Yield: 4 servings
Dietary Notes: Gluten Free

Mexico's cuisine is famous for the culinary traditions at its seaports around the country, including Veracruz, Mazatlán, and Acapulco. Shrimp is abundant there, and this recipe combines it with the vibrant flavors of chile, garlic, tomato, cumin, and cilantro.

1 pound shrimp, peeled and deveined

Salt

Freshly ground black pepper

2 Roma tomatoes

¼ white onion, peeled and left whole

1 garlic clove, unpeeled

2 canned chipotle chiles in adobo

½ teaspoon dried Mexican oregano

⅛ teaspoon ground cumin

2 tablespoons unsalted butter

½ lime, juiced

Chopped cilantro, to garnish

1. Season the shrimp with a pinch of salt and pepper, coat evenly, and set aside in the refrigerator.

2. Move the oven rack to the top position, and preheat the broiler on high.

3. Line a small baking sheet with aluminum foil, and place the tomatoes, onion, and garlic clove on the baking sheet. Add the baking sheet to the broiler, and char evenly on all sides; remove the garlic after 4 to 5 minutes, and remove the onion and tomato after 8 to 10 minutes.

4. When the garlic is slightly cooled, peel the garlic and put all charred ingredients in a blender with the chipotle chiles, oregano, and cumin. Purée until very smooth; then set aside.

5. Warm a large pan over medium-high heat. Add the butter and, once it starts sizzling, add the shrimp. Sauté the shrimp in the butter until they start to become pink, about 1 minute. Pour the puréed sauce into the pan, and cook for another 5 minutes, or until the sauce thickens slightly and the shrimp are fully cooked.

6. Add a generous pinch of salt, the lime juice, and chopped cilantro, and serve immediately.

Barbacoa de Pollo

Chicken Barbacoa

Difficulty: Medium
Prep Time: 20 minutes
(plus 20 minutes wait time)
Cook Time: 1½ hours
Yield: 6 servings
Dietary Notes: Dairy Free,
Gluten Free

Many *tortillerías*, like the one seen in Santa Cecilia in *Coco*, not only make and sell corn dough for tortillas, but also often sell *barbacoa*—a spiced meat dish that's traditionally slow roasted for hours in an underground pit. This recipe has the classic flavor of barbacoa, but it's modified so you can easily prepare it in a home oven. In the movie, Miguel runs right past La Tortillería in his hurry to get back home and replace Héctor's photo on the family altar and get Mama Coco to remember Héctor before he vanishes forever!

10 guajillo chiles, stemmed and seeded

10 garlic cloves

1 white onion, roughly chopped

One 3-inch Mexican cinnamon stick

2 tablespoons dried Mexican oregano

½ teaspoon black peppercorns

½ teaspoon cumin seed

3 cloves

2 bay leaves

½ pound Roma tomatoes, quartered

¼ pound tomatillos, husked, rinsed, and halved

1 tablespoon salt

4 pounds chicken breast and leg pieces, bone in and skin on

10 dried avocado leaves

SPECIALTY TOOLS

Spice grinder, molcajete, or mortar and pestle

1. Preheat the oven to 375°F.

2. Bring 5 cups of water to a boil in a medium pot, and add the chiles. Turn off the heat, and let the chiles soak for 20 minutes until they are rehydrated and soft. Transfer them to a blender along with ½ cup of the soaking liquid, and set aside.

3. Warm a large pan over medium heat. Add the garlic and onion, and toast evenly for about 5 to 7 minutes, stirring occasionally. Remove the garlic and onion, and set aside; then add the cinnamon, oregano, pepper, cumin, cloves, and bay leaves to the pan, and toast until fragrant, about 2 minutes. Add the toasted spices to a spice grinder, *molcajete*, or mortar and pestle, and process until very finely ground; then set aside.

4. Add the tomatoes and tomatillos to a small pot with ¼ cup water. Bring to a boil over medium-high heat; then reduce heat to medium-low and simmer for 15 minutes, until the tomatillos are darker in color.

5. To the blender with the chiles, add the tomatoes, tomatillos, and any remaining water in the pot, along with the garlic, onion, ground spices, and salt. Purée the mixture until very smooth.

6. Using a 5-quart Dutch oven or another heavy-bottomed pot with a lid, add the chicken pieces. Pour the puréed sauce over the chicken, and add the avocado leaves. Mix everything together to make sure the sauce covers all parts of the chicken. Cover the pot with a tight-fitting lid, and bake for about 1 hour, until the thickest part of the leg meat reaches an internal temperature of 165°F using a food thermometer.

7. Remove the chicken from the oven, and let it rest for a few minutes before serving.

NOTE:

Tender young goat, lamb, and beef are common meats used for barbacoa, but bone-in chicken can be easier to find and cooks in a fraction of the time without sacrificing flavor.

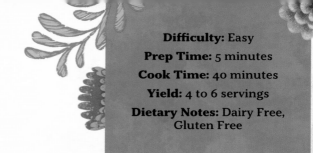

Tinga de Pollo y Chorizo

Chicken and Chorizo Tinga

Difficulty: Easy
Prep Time: 5 minutes
Cook Time: 40 minutes
Yield: 4 to 6 servings
Dietary Notes: Dairy Free, Gluten Free

In *Coco*, Héctor is taunted with the nickname "Chorizo" because he's told he died from eating this spiced sausage. He is quick to correct them by saying that he died of food poisoning, which is "very different." The actual reason he came to be in the Land of the Dead is much more complicated than that. After he learns the truth, maybe he'll be able to enjoy chorizo again.

6 Roma tomatoes

2 tomatillos, husked and rinsed

2 chipotle chiles in adobo plus 1 tablespoon adobo sauce

½ teaspoon dried Mexican oregano

¼ teaspoon dried marjoram

¼ teaspoon dried thyme

1½ teaspoons kosher salt

¼ teaspoon freshly ground black pepper

1 tablespoon vegetable oil

6 ounces Mexican chorizo, crumbled into large pieces or chopped

½ white onion, sliced

3 garlic cloves, minced

3 to 4 poached skinless, boneless chicken breasts (prepared according to Pollo en Mole Rojo recipe on page 67), shredded

2 avocados, sliced

1. Put the tomatoes and tomatillos in a saucepan, and cover them with water. Bring to a boil over high heat; then reduce to medium-high heat and simmer for 8 to 10 minutes, until the tomatoes and tomatillos are soft but not falling apart.

2. Place cooked tomatoes and tomatillos in a blender, along with the chipotle chiles and sauce, oregano, marjoram, thyme, salt, and pepper, and purée until very smooth. Set aside.

3. In a large pan, heat the oil over medium heat. Add the chorizo, and fry until the meat is cooked, about 5 minutes, breaking up any large pieces with a spatula. The chorizo will render its own fat while cooking, so remove all but 2 tablespoons of oil from the pan. Add the onion and garlic, and sauté until the onions are softened, 5 minutes.

4. Pour in the tomato sauce, and simmer, stirring occasionally, until the color darkens, about 10 minutes. You can partially cover the pan with a lid to contain the splatter.

5. Add the shredded chicken to the sauce; let cook until the chicken absorbs the sauce, 5 minutes. Serve warm with avocado slices.

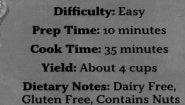

Difficulty: Easy
Prep Time: 10 minutes
Cook Time: 35 minutes
Yield: About 4 cups
Dietary Notes: Dairy Free, Gluten Free, Contains Nuts

Picadillo

Spiced Beef Hash

This sautéed and stewed ground meat dish can take many forms. Some people make it with just a few spices and potatoes; others dress it up with the help of olives, capers, raisins, and nuts. This recipe takes the latter approach, which gives the picadillo more complex flavor and texture. Serve it warm with rice, or let the mixture cool to use in tamales and chiles rellenos.

2 tablespoons vegetable oil

½ large white onion, finely chopped

3 garlic cloves, finely chopped

1 pound ground beef, 20% fat

¾ teaspoon kosher salt

½ teaspoon freshly ground black pepper

¼ teaspoon ground cinnamon

¼ teaspoon ground allspice

⅛ teaspoon ground clove

1 pound ripe tomatoes, chopped, or one 15-ounce can crushed tomatoes

¼ cup slivered almonds

¼ cup diced pimiento-stuffed green olives

3 tablespoons capers, drained

3 tablespoons raisins

1. Warm the oil in a large skillet over medium-high heat. Add the onion, and cook until translucent and softened, about 5 minutes.

2. Add the garlic, and cook for another minute; then stir in the meat, salt, pepper, cinnamon, allspice, and clove. Using a wooden or silicone spatula, break up the ground meat; cook until the meat is cooked and most of the liquid has cooked off, about 10 minutes.

3. Stir in the tomatoes, and cook until softened, about 10 minutes.

4. Add the almonds, olives, capers, and raisins; cook for another 10 minutes.

5. The mixture should be a thicker stew consistency but not wet. If needed, continue simmering to cook off excess moisture. Serve warm.

Pollo Adobado

Adobo Roasted Chicken

Difficulty: Medium

Prep Time: 15 minutes (plus 3 hours wait time)

Cook Time: 1 hour and 15 minutes

Yield: 4 to 6 servings

Dietary Notes: Dairy Free, Gluten Free

Dante follows Miguel everywhere he goes, even when Miguel tries to steal Ernesto de la Cruz's famous guitar so he can perform in the talent contest against his family's wishes. To distract Dante from ruining the plan, Miguel grabs a chicken leg from another gravesite and throws it off into the distance. If the chicken leg were marinated in this spiced three-chile adobo, you would chase after it, too.

---

4 pounds mixed drumsticks or legs, preferably bone in and skin on

4 teaspoons kosher salt, divided, plus more to taste

2 Roma tomatoes, cored

½ white onion, whole, plus 1 large white onion, cut into a 1-inch dice

4 garlic cloves, unpeeled, plus 8 garlic cloves, peeled and smashed, divided

4 guajillo chiles, stemmed and seeded

2 morita chiles, stemmed and seeded

2 ancho chiles, stemmed and seeded

One 3-inch Mexican cinnamon stick

2 bay leaves

1 teaspoon black peppercorns

1 teaspoon cumin seeds

2 teaspoons dried Mexican oregano

¼ cup white vinegar

2 to 3 Yukon gold potatoes, cut into wedges

2 to 3 large carrots, cut into 1-inch pieces

2 tablespoons extra virgin olive oil

Freshly ground black pepper

Lime wedges, for serving

---

1. Pat dry all the chicken, and trim off any excess skin or fat. Sprinkle generously and evenly with 2 teaspoons salt. Cover the chicken, and put it back in the refrigerator while preparing the adobo marinade.

2. Warm a large sauté pan over medium heat. When hot, add the whole tomatoes, ½ onion, and 4 unpeeled garlic cloves. Char the ingredients evenly on all sides: 4 to 5 minutes for the garlic, and 8 to 10 minutes for the tomatoes and onion. When the garlic is slightly cooled, peel the garlic and set everything aside.

3. Add the guajillo, morita, and ancho chiles, and toast until fragrant, 1 minute. Add the cinnamon, bay leaves, peppercorns, cumin seeds, and oregano, and toast until fragrant, 1 minute. Add the 4 unpeeled garlic and 2 cups of water, and bring to a simmer for 15 minutes.

4. Transfer to a blender. Add the vinegar and remaining 2 teaspoons salt, and then purée on high speed until the mixture is very smooth. Remove the chicken from the refrigerator, and

pour the adobo through a fine-mesh strainer directly over the chicken. Spread the adobo evenly both over and under the skin of the chicken. Place it back in the fridge for a couple hours, preferably overnight.

5. One hour before cooking, pull the chicken from the refrigerator and preheat the oven to 425°F.

6. Place the chicken pieces on a baking sheet. In a mixing bowl, add the 8 smashed garlic cloves, potatoes, carrots, and diced onion, and toss with the oil, a generous pinch of salt, and black pepper.

7. Place the vegetables around the chicken, and roast until the sauce darkens, the chicken looks crispy, and the thickest part of the drumstick reaches an internal temperature of 165°F, about 30 to 45 minutes.

8. If the chicken is a golden brown color but hasn't reached the right temperature, cover it loosely with aluminum foil and continue cooking.

9. Let the chicken rest for 15 minutes before serving; then portion the chicken and vegetables to plates with lime wedges for garnishing.

Pollo en Mole Rojo

Chicken in Red Mole

Difficulty: Advanced
Prep Time: 20 minutes
(plus up to 24 hours wait time)
Cook Time: 2 hours
Yield: 8 to 10 servings
Dietary Notes: Dairy Free,
Contains Nuts

The Mexican state of Oaxaca and its capitol of the same name are famous for their variety of moles. These complex and colorful sauces adorn simply prepared meats or vegetables and act as a centerpiece for many of the region's festivities. Though every recipe can be slightly different, the recognizable flavors and techniques in this iconic mole will transport you to this beautiful region.

POACHED CHICKEN

1 white onion, halved

5 garlic cloves, crushed

2 bay leaves

1 tablespoon kosher salt

½ teaspoon black peppercorns

8 boneless, skinless chicken breasts

MOLE

2 ounces guajillo chiles, stemmed and seeded

4 ounces mulato chiles, stemmed and seeded

4 ounces ancho chiles, stemmed and seeded

⅔ cup sesame seeds

¼ cup pine nuts

½ cup raw almonds

¼ cup raw peanuts

3 tablespoons pepitas

2 Roma tomatoes, cored and quartered

2 tomatillos, husked, rinsed, and quartered

¼ teaspoon aniseed

¼ teaspoon cumin seeds

½ teaspoon black peppercorns

2 allspice berries

2 cloves

One 2-inch piece Mexican cinnamon

2 bay leaves

1 tablespoon dried Mexican oregano

1 teaspoon fresh thyme

¼ cup vegetable oil, plus more if needed

½ white onion, roughly chopped

3 large garlic cloves

1 cup peeled and chopped sweet apple, such as Honeycrisp or Gala

1 very ripe (black) plantain, peeled and chopped

¼ cup raisins

4 ounces fluffy white bread, such as challah or dinner rolls

6 cups chicken stock, divided

4 ounces semisweet Mexican chocolate

1½ tablespoons kosher salt

Toasted sesame seeds, for garnishing

SPECIALTY TOOLS

Spice grinder, molcajete, or mortar and pestle

TO MAKE THE POACHED CHICKEN:

1. In a large pot, bring 1 gallon (4 quarts) of water and the onion, garlic, bay leaves, salt, and peppercorns to a simmer over medium heat. Add the chicken, and bring back to a simmer; cover partially, and cook for 12 to 15 minutes, depending on the size of the chicken pieces. Turn off the heat, and let the chicken cool in the broth. Strain the broth into a large bowl, and reserve for making the mole.

TO MAKE THE MOLE:

2. Preheat the oven to 375°F. Keeping all three types of chiles separated, place them on a large baking sheet and toast them in the oven, turning them halfway to toast evenly. Remove the guajillo chiles after 3 minutes, the mulato chiles after 5 minutes, and the ancho chiles after 8 minutes. Add the chiles to a heatproof bowl, and cover with boiling water to rehydrate and soften the chiles for 30 minutes.

3. Place the sesame seeds, pine nuts, almonds, peanuts, and pepitas on the same baking sheet, and put in the oven for 5 to 7 minutes, until lightly browned and aromatic. Set aside.

4. In a medium ungreased sauce pan, add the tomatoes, tomatillos, and ¾ cup of water. Cook over medium heat for 15 minutes or until the tomatillos start to darken in color but are not mushy. Take off heat and set aside.

5. In a large ungreased sauté pan over medium heat, add the aniseed, cumin, peppercorns, allspice, cloves, cinnamon stick, and bay leaves. Toast until fragrant, 1 minute, stirring the pan every few seconds to prevent the spices from burning. Add the toasted spices to a spice grinder or mortar and pestle along with the oregano and thyme, and grind until very fine. Set aside the spice mix.

6. To the same large sauté pan, warm the vegetable oil over medium heat, and sauté the onions and garlic until they are translucent, about 5 minutes. Remove the onion and garlic from the pan, and place in a mixing bowl.

7. Next, add the apple and plantain, and fry until golden brown and crispy, about 8 minutes; then transfer to the mixing bowl with the onions and garlic.

8. Add the raisins to the pan, and fry for 5 minutes, adding a little more vegetable oil if the pan is too dry. Then transfer the raisins to the mixing bowl.

9. Add the bread, and toast in whatever oil is left in the pan until golden brown; then transfer to the bowl.

10. In batches, add all the ingredients to a blender, and purée until very smooth: the drained tomatoes and tomatillos, rehydrated chiles, toasted nuts and seeds, ground spices, and all the fried ingredients. To help the blender blades catch and pull in all the ingredients, add up to 2 cups chicken stock.

11. Strain the mole paste through a fine-mesh strainer into a soup pot, and bring to a simmer over medium heat, stirring frequently to prevent the mole from burning.

12. Add the chocolate, salt, and remaining chicken stock, and continue simmering for at least another 20 minutes and up to several hours. The consistency should be loose enough to pour from a ladle but not watery.

13. Taste and adjust the seasoning, to ensure that it tastes well balanced. The flavor of the mole improves after 24 hours of marinating in the refrigerator.

14. To serve, place a cooked chicken breast on a plate with a ladle of mole and a sprinkle of toasted sesame seeds.

Albóndigas al Chipotle

Meatballs in Tomato-Chipotle Sauce

Difficulty: Medium
Prep Time: 25 minutes
Cook Time: 30 minutes
Yield: 4 to 6 servings
Dietary Notes: Dairy Free

Did your family members crave *albóndigas* when they were alive? This comfort food of juicy meatballs cooked in a smoky tomato sauce, served with slices of avocado and a warm bowl of Arroz Blanco (page 83), will welcome any ancestor home.

CHIPOTLE SAUCE

8 Roma tomatoes, cored

2 tablespoons vegetable oil

1 white onion, chopped

1 garlic clove, chopped

3 canned chipotles in adobo sauce, sauce reserved

2 teaspoons kosher salt

Pinch of freshly ground black pepper

MEATBALLS

1 pound ground beef, 20% fat

1 pound ground pork, 20% fat

1 cup panko breadcrumbs

½ cup parsley leaves, chopped

½ cup minced white onion, or grated on the large holes of a box grater

3 garlic cloves, grated finely and divided

1 teaspoon dried Mexican oregano

2 teaspoons kosher salt

Pinch of freshly ground black pepper

2 eggs, whisked together

2 tablespoons vegetable oil

TO MAKE THE CHIPOTLE SAUCE:

1. Warm an ungreased large pan or Dutch oven over medium-high heat. Add the tomatoes, and char evenly on all sides, turning occasionally, for about 10 minutes. Transfer the tomatoes to a blender, and set aside.

2. To the same pan, add the vegetable oil; warm over medium heat. Add the chopped onion and garlic, and sauté until translucent, 5 minutes; then add to the blender with the tomatoes along with any leftover oil.

3. To the blender, add the chipotles, 2 tablespoons of reserved adobo sauce, salt, and pepper, and purée on medium speed until smooth. Set sauce aside while preparing the meatballs.

TO MAKE THE MEATBALLS:

4. In a large bowl, add the ground beef and pork. Break apart the blocks of meat, being careful not to overwork it—too much handling, and the meatballs will be dense and chewy.

5. In a smaller bowl, mix together the breadcrumbs, parsley, minced onion, grated garlic, oregano, salt, and pepper. Add the breadcrumb mixture to the ground meat, pour in the whisked eggs, and very gently mix the ingredients together. Form roughly ¼-cup-size meatballs, and arrange them on a baking sheet or large plate.

6. Add oil to a large skillet over medium-high heat. Working in batches, put the meatballs into the pan and brown them on all sides, turning occasionally, for about 5 minutes. As they finish cooking, remove the meatballs from the pan and set them aside on a clean plate.

7. When all meatballs are seared, drain all but 1 tablespoon of fat from the skillet. Pour the tomato sauce into the skillet, and bring the sauce to a boil over medium-high heat. Add the seared meatballs to the skillet, reduce heat to medium, cover, and cook for 10 minutes. Uncover the pan, and continue simmering for another 10 minutes to reduce the sauce slightly.

8. Meatballs can be stored in an airtight container in the refrigerator for 5 days.

Pozole Rojo

Red Pozole

Difficulty: Medium
Prep Time: 20 minutes
(plus 20 minutes wait time)
Cook Time: 1¼ hours
(plus 3 hours, depending on protein choice)
Yield: 12 servings
Dietary Notes: Dairy Free, Gluten Free

This iconic dish of indigenous origins is beloved to this day in all its many forms. You'll immediately recognize this mainstay of Mexican cuisine by its steaming chilied broth and intensely aromatic cumin, oregano, and clove. Because of the dish's popularity, it is possible that Miguel's family would make pozole, too, but since every recipe is slightly different, they'd likely have their own special touches. Chicken is a great substitute for the more traditional pork when you want a pozole that is lighter and quick to cook.

3 pounds bone-in and skin-on chicken hindquarters, or pork shoulder cut into 2-inch cubes

1 medium white onion, peeled and halved, plus ½ white onion, divided

1 head garlic, halved horizontally, plus 3 garlic cloves, divided

2 bay leaves

8 sprigs cilantro

1 tablespoon plus 1 pinch kosher salt, divided

Three 25-ounce cans hominy, drained and rinsed

6 guajillo chiles, stemmed and seeded

2 árbol chiles, stemmed and seeded

1 teaspoon cumin seeds

2 whole cloves

1 tablespoon dried Mexican oregano

GARNISHES

Romaine lettuce, finely chopped

Avocados, sliced

1 bunch radishes, thinly sliced

1 cup dried Mexican oregano

8 limes, cut into wedges

1 onion, finely chopped

3 serrano chiles, finely sliced`

1. Place the chicken or pork in a large soup pot. Add enough water to cover the top of the meat by at least 2 inches; then add the halved onion, garlic head, bay leaves, cilantro sprigs, and 1 tablespoon of salt.

2. Bring the water to a boil over high heat; then cover and reduce the heat to medium, cooking the meat until fork-tender: 20 to 25 minutes for chicken and 2 to 2½ hours for pork.

3. Remove the meat from the water, and let cool. Remove the skin and bones from the chicken, shred the meat into bite-size pieces, and reserve. Discard the onion, garlic, cilantro, and bay leaves from the stock, and set aside.

4. To the stock, add the hominy and 2 more cups of water. Bring to a boil over high heat; then reduce heat to medium, and let simmer gently for 30 minutes.

5. Put the guajillo and árbol chiles in a heatproof container, and soak them in boiling water for 20 minutes. To a blender, add the remaining ½ onion, remaining 3 garlic cloves, cumin, cloves, oregano, a generous pinch of salt, and ½ cup of the stock; purée until smooth on high speed for at least 1 minute. Strain the purée through a fine-mesh strainer into the pot with the stock and hominy.

6. Add the shredded meat to the pot, and let simmer for another 20 to 30 minutes. Taste and adjust the salt, as needed. Serve in large soup bowls along with the garnishes of your choice.

Cerdo en Mole Verde

Pork in Green Mole

Difficulty: Medium
Prep Time: 20 minutes
Cook Time: 3 hours 15 minutes
Yield: 6 to 8 servings
Dietary Notes: Dairy Free, Gluten Free

Just before going on stage at Plaza de la Cruz, Miguel tries overcoming his stage fright by letting out his best *grito*. Unfortunately, it sounds a bit weak and doesn't inspire confidence in Héctor that he can win the contest. Only when he's on stage in front of an audience does Miguel let out a truly impressive grito that launches him into his song. You'll let out your own grito when you taste this hearty stew. Its characteristic flavor comes from an herb called *hoja santa* (sacred leaf), which gives the dish a unique and subtle anise flavor. Dried hoja santa can be easier to find in markets and online, so this recipe includes it as a substitute.

4 pounds pork shoulder or boneless country-style pork ribs, with excess fat removed, cut into 2-inch pieces

1 head garlic, halved horizontally

1 white onion, halved horizontally

3 bay leaves

1 tablespoon whole black peppercorns

2 tablespoons kosher salt, divided

2 cups dried navy beans, rinsed, or four 15-ounce cans navy beans, drained and rinsed

MOLE

2 pounds tomatillos, husked and rinsed

2 serrano chiles, stemmed and roughly chopped

3 garlic cloves

½ cup white onion, chopped

1½ teaspoons ground cumin

¼ cup masa harina or ½ pound fresh masa

1 teaspoon kosher salt, plus more to taste

¼ teaspoon freshly ground black pepper

1 cup epazote leaves, chopped (or substitute cilantro)

1 cup parsley leaves and tender stems, chopped

3 to 4 hoja santa leaves, torn, or 1 teaspoon crumbled dried hoja santa

1. Add the pork, garlic, onion, bay leaves, peppercorns, and 1 tablespoon salt to a large pot, and cover with water (at least 8 cups). Bring to a rolling boil over high heat; then reduce heat to medium, and cover the pot with a lid. Let cook for 1½ to 2 hours, until the pork falls apart easily. Remove the meat from the pot; then strain and reserve the pork broth.

2. Skip this step if you are using canned beans. Combine the dried beans in a large pot, and add enough water to cover them by at least 3 inches. Bring the water to a boil over high heat; then reduce heat to medium, and cover partially. Cook the beans for at least 1 hour, or until they are tender but not falling apart. Season the beans with 1 teaspoon of the remaining salt at a time until the bean broth tastes well seasoned and not overly salty. Continue simmering gently for another 15 to 30 minutes. Strain and reserve the beans, reserving the bean broth for another recipe.

TO MAKE THE MOLE:

3. Add the tomatillos, serrano chiles, garlic, onion, cumin, and 1 cup of the reserved pork broth to a blender. Blend until smooth, and then add it to a large pot.

4. Add the masa, salt, and black pepper to the blender along with 1 cup of the reserved pork broth; blend until smooth. Add another 2 cups of broth, and continue blending until thoroughly combined.

5. Add the puréed masa mixture to the pot. Bring the pot to a simmer over medium-high heat; let cook for 15 minutes, stirring constantly so that the masa doesn't burn to the bottom of the pot.

6. Meanwhile, add the epazote, parsley, and hoja santa to the blender along with 1 cup of reserved broth, and blend until smooth. Add this to the mole pot along with the reserved cooked beans and pork, and let simmer for another 20 minutes, stirring occasionally to prevent the sauce from burning.

7. Taste and adjust seasonings, as needed. Serve warm in large soup bowls.

Chicharrones en Salsa Verde

Pork Rinds in Green Salsa

Difficulty: Easy
Prep Time: 10 minutes
Cook Time: 30 minutes
Yield: 4 servings
Dietary Notes: Dairy Free, Gluten Free

Héctor's friend Chicharrón is quickly vanishing because fewer people in the Land of the Living remember who he was. To comfort his friend in the moments before his transition, Héctor sings Chicharrón a song with the guitar that Miguel eventually uses to enter the talent competition at Plaza de la Cruz. This popular stewed dish uses fried pork rinds in tribute to a great friend, Chicharrón.

SALSA VERDE

1½ pounds tomatillos, husked and rinsed

2 cups water, chicken stock, or vegetable stock, plus ½ cup reserved

1 serrano pepper, stemmed

2 garlic cloves

½ white onion, chopped

1 teaspoon cumin seeds

½ cup chopped cilantro

1 sprig epazote, chopped

Kosher salt

CHICHARRONES

1 tablespoon vegetable oil

¼ white onion, sliced

6 ounces chicharrones with some meat attached, broken up into 1-inch pieces

Kosher salt

Chopped cilantro, for garnishing

12 corn tortillas, homemade (page 26) or good-quality store bought, warmed

TO MAKE THE SALSA VERDE:

1. Combine the tomatillos, 2 cups of water or stock, serrano pepper, garlic, onion, and cumin seeds in a large saucepan, and bring to a boil. Reduce heat to medium, cover, and simmer until the onion has softened, about 15 minutes.

2. Add all the contents from the saucepan to a blender, along with the cilantro, epazote, and a generous pinch of kosher salt; and purée until smooth. Taste and adjust salt, as needed.

TO MAKE THE CHICHARRONES:

3. Heat the vegetable oil in a large sauté pan over medium-high heat. Add the onion, and fry gently without browning for 2 minutes.

4. To the pan, add the blended Salsa Verde, stirring occasionally until the salsa has thickened slightly and is a shade darker, about 5 minutes. If the salsa is too thick, stir in reserved stock and bring it back to a simmer.

5. Add the chicharrones and a pinch of salt, and continue cooking over medium heat until the chicharrones soften, between 5 and 10 minutes.

6. Garnish with chopped cilantro and serve with warm corn tortillas.

NOTE

Buy chicharrones at meat counters where they are kept warm; these are likely fresher and more flavorful. *Chicharrones botaneros* are the shelf-stable snacking chicharrones and don't have as much meaty flavor or texture for this dish.

Sopa de Milpa

Cornfield Soup

Difficulty: Easy
Prep Time: 25 minutes
Cook Time: 30 minutes
Yield: 6 servings
Dietary Notes: Vegetarian, Gluten Free

A *milpa* is an ancient farming system that farmers and families still use to grow crops such as corn, squash, and beans, among others. The crops that are grown are chosen because they help nourish the soil and sustain the plants as they grow. This recipe features some traditional ingredients that are commonly grown together. You can customize your *sopa* with more vegetables, such as cooked fava beans, carrots, baby potatoes, green beans, and tomatoes.

2 poblano chiles

1 tablespoon vegetable oil

2 tablespoons unsalted butter

1 white onion, finely diced

3 garlic cloves, finely diced

2 zucchini squash, diced

12 squash flowers, stamens removed

2 ears fresh corn, cut into large chunks, or 2½ cups corn kernels

1 sprig fresh epazote

8 cups vegetable or chicken stock

Kosher salt

1½ cups queso fresco, crumbled and divided

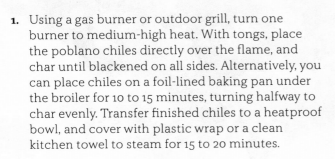

1. Using a gas burner or outdoor grill, turn one burner to medium-high heat. With tongs, place the poblano chiles directly over the flame, and char until blackened on all sides. Alternatively, you can place chiles on a foil-lined baking pan under the broiler for 10 to 15 minutes, turning halfway to char evenly. Transfer finished chiles to a heatproof bowl, and cover with plastic wrap or a clean kitchen towel to steam for 15 to 20 minutes.

2. When the chiles have cooled, remove the blistered skins, seeds, and stems. Slice the chiles into thin strips, and set aside.

3. In a medium pan, heat the oil and butter over medium heat, and add the onion. When the onion starts to soften, after about 5 minutes, add the garlic; cook for another minute. Add the zucchini, squash flowers, corn, epazote, and stock. Bring back to a simmer, and let cook for 10 minutes.

4. Add poblano chile pieces, and season with salt, to taste. Serve warm with ¼ cup of crumbled queso fresco in each bowl.

Birria de Res

Spiced Beef Stew

Difficulty: Medium
Prep Time: 10 minutes (plus overnight wait time)
Cook Time: 3½ hours
Yield: 10 to 12 servings
Dietary Notes: Dairy Free, Gluten Free

Slow-braised meat in aromatic spices and chiles is the key to a delicious birria. For the best flavor, start the meat marinade the day before you plan to cook. After that, birria *is* essentially a hands-off dish.

2 to 3 pounds beef short ribs

2 to 3 pounds chuck roast, cut into large chunks

2 tablespoons kosher salt

10 dried guajillo chiles

4 cloves garlic

2 whole cloves

1 tablespoon sesame seeds

One 3-inch Mexican cinnamon stick

2 teaspoons whole black peppercorns

4 bay leaves

2 teaspoons dried Mexican oregano

2 teaspoons dried thyme

½ teaspoon ground cumin

½ teaspoon ground ginger

1 tablespoon apple cider vinegar

1 large white onion, finely diced, for garnishing

2 cups fresh cilantro, chopped, for garnishing

12 corn tortillas, homemade (page 26) or good-quality store bought, warmed

Lime wedges, for garnishing

1. The day before you plan to serve the birria, season the short ribs and chuck roast with the salt and let it sit while preparing the marinade. For convenience, put the meat in a large dish that fits in your refrigerator and can go in the oven, such as a Dutch oven or a large heavy-bottomed pot with a lid.

2. Heat an ungreased large sauté pan over medium heat, and toast the chiles on all sides until fragrant, 1 minute. Remove the chiles and set them aside. Add the garlic, cloves, sesame seeds, cinnamon, and peppercorns, and toast until fragrant, 2 minutes.

3. Add the bay leaves, oregano, thyme, cumin, ginger, and 4 cups of water and bring to a boil on high heat. Reduce heat to medium, and let simmer vigorously for 10 minutes.

4. Turn off the heat, and transfer all contents from the pan to a blender; add the vinegar and purée on high speed until smooth. Let the marinade cool to room temperature, then pour the marinade over the meat, cover with a lid or plastic wrap, and refrigerate for at least 4 hours, preferably overnight.

5. Pull the marinated meat out of the refrigerator an hour before cooking, and preheat the oven to 350°F. Add enough fresh water to barely cover the meat; then place the lid on the pot, and roast in the oven for 3 hours.

6. Test the meat to be sure it's very tender and shreds easily when pulled. If not, continue roasting longer. Remove from the oven, and let cool slightly before serving.

7. Portion meat into soup bowls with a ladle or two of broth, garnish with diced white onion and cilantro, and serve with warmed tortillas and lime wedges.

NOTE

For a more traditional birria, use the same proportion of bone-in lamb shoulder, ribs, or legs, and roast for the same amount of time.

Sopa de Tortilla

Tortilla Soup

Difficulty: Medium
Prep Time: 10 minutes
(plus 20 minutes wait time)
Cook Time: 40 minutes
Yield: 6 servings
Dietary Notes: Vegetarian,
Vegan, Dairy Free, Gluten Free

Freshly made corn tortillas are soft, pliable, and perfect for tacos or as an accompaniment to a main meal. Day-old homemade tortillas, however, can be slightly brittle and hard to bend. Channel the quick thinking and resourcefulness of the Rivera family matriarchs by cutting up your old tortillas and frying them to use atop this delicious sopa. A generous amount and variety of garnishes is what makes this dish magical, so don't skimp on the toppings.

3 dried pasilla chiles, stemmed and seeded

4 Roma tomatoes

½ white onion

2 garlic cloves, unpeeled

6 to 8 cups chicken or vegetable stock, divided

2 tablespoons plus ¼ cup vegetable oil, divided

1 large sprig fresh epazote

12 corn tortillas, cut into thin strips

GARNISHES

Cooked and shredded chicken

Pasilla chile, cut into rings and fried for 8 to 10 seconds

Queso fresco, crumbled (optional)

Mexican crema

Lime, cut into wedges

Avocado, diced

Cilantro, chopped

1. Warm a large ungreased pan over medium heat. When the pan is hot, add the pasilla chiles, and toast for about 1 minute on each side, being careful not to burn them.

2. Transfer the chiles to a heatproof container, and cover with boiling water; let them soak for 20 minutes. Strain the chiles, and discard the soaking liquid. Add the rehydrated chiles to a blender, and set them aside.

3. To the same warmed pan, add the whole tomatoes, onion, and garlic cloves. Char the ingredients evenly on all sides: 4 to 5 minutes for the garlic, and 8 to 10 minutes for the tomato and onion. When cool enough to handle, peel the garlic and add all the charred ingredients to a blender along with 1 cup of chicken stock. Purée the mixture until it is completely smooth. Strain the purée through a fine mesh strainer into a large bowl, and reserve.

4. Warm 2 tablespoons of oil in a large sauce pot over medium heat. When the oil is hot, carefully pour the tomato purée into the pan, and partially cover it to contain the splatter. Simmer the sauce for 10 minutes until it darkens and thickens slightly. Add 5 cups of stock and the epazote and let simmer uncovered for another 10 minutes while you prepare the fried tortillas.

5. For the tortillas, add ¼ cup of oil to a small pan or pot on medium heat. Fry the tortilla strips in batches, being careful not to overcrowd the pan. The tortilla strips cook in less than 1 minute and continue to cook after they're removed from the oil, so transfer them to a paper towel–lined plate when they start to become golden.

6. If you're using fried pasilla chile rings as a garnish, add the sliced chiles to the oil after you finish the tortilla strips. Transfer the rings to the paper towel-lined plate to absorb excess oil.

7. Taste the soup and adjust as needed: If the flavors are too intense, add another cup of remaining stock to balance. To serve, ladle 1 cup of soup to every bowl, and add generous amounts of the fried tortilla strips and other garnishes, to your liking.

Guarniciones

ACCOMPANIMENTS

Difficulty: Easy
Prep Time: 5 minutes
Cook Time: 1 to 1½ hours
Yield: 4 cups
Dietary Notes: Vegan, Dairy Free, Gluten Free

Frijoles de la Olla

Simple Pot Beans

Many families start the morning by cooking a pot of beans to have for lunch and dinner. This basic recipe can be used for any kind of bean, although black beans are the most commonly used. If you don't soak the beans beforehand, simply add another 30 to 45 minutes to the total cook time.

½ pound dried black, pinto, or white beans, rinsed and soaked overnight

3 cloves garlic, smashed

½ white onion, halved vertically through the stem

3 sprigs fresh epazote or 1 dried bay leaf

2 teaspoons kosher salt

1. In a large pot, add the beans, garlic, onion, and epazote. Cover the beans with 3 inches of water, and bring to a boil. Lower heat to medium-low, cover the pot with a lid, and cook until the beans are tender, 1 to 1½ hours.

2. Check the beans halfway through, and add water as needed to keep the beans covered.

3. When the beans are cooked, add salt and remove the pot from the heat. Discard the onion and garlic.

USING A PRESSURE COOKER OR INSTANT POT

1. Add the beans, garlic, onion, epazote, and salt to the pressure cooker, and cover the beans with 3 inches of water. Using the high pressure cook setting, set a 30 minute timer; let the pressure release slowly when finished, about 20 additional minutes after the cook setting finishes. If beans are not fully cooked, secure the lid, seal the release valve, and continue cooking for 10 more minutes.

Arroz Blanco

Mexican White Rice

Difficulty: Easy
Prep Time: 5 minutes
Cook Time: 25 minutes
Yield: 6 to 8 servings
Dietary Notes: Vegetarian, Vegan, Dairy Free, Gluten Free

Side dishes in Mexican cuisine round out any meal. Without them, an important piece of a puzzle is missing—like the torn corner of an old photo that could alter a certain family's ban on music and a certain young boy's perspective on a former idol.

2 tablespoons vegetable oil

¼ white onion, finely chopped

3 garlic cloves, minced

1½ cups long-grain white rice, rinsed until water runs clear

3 cups hot stock (chicken or vegetable) or water

Juice of ½ lime (about 1 tablespoon)

1 teaspoon kosher salt

4 sprigs parsley

1. In a large pan with a lid, heat the oil, onion, and garlic over medium heat. When the garlic starts to sizzle, add the rice, stirring constantly, and fry until translucent, 4 to 5 minutes.

2. Add the hot stock or water, lime juice, and salt. When the liquid simmers steadily, add the parsley sprigs, cover the pan, reduce the heat to medium-low, and cook for 12 minutes.

3. Remove the pan from the heat, and let it sit for 10 minutes undisturbed. Remove the lid, fluff the grains with a fork, and serve immediately.

Arroz Rojo

Mexican Red Rice

Difficulty: Easy
Prep Time: 10 minutes
Cook Time: 25 minutes
Yield: 6 to 8 servings
Dietary Notes: Vegetarian, Vegan, Dairy Free, Gluten Free

A steamy pot of freshly cooked rice is a must-have in any kitchen. It's the perfect accompaniment to dishes such as rich and complex moles. It's also tasty on its own, simply topped with a fried egg for breakfast.

2¼ cups stock (chicken or vegetable) or water

5 tablespoons tomato paste

2 teaspoons kosher salt

⅓ teaspoon freshly ground black pepper

4 teaspoons vegetable oil

1 small white onion, chopped

4 garlic cloves, thinly sliced

1½ cups long-grain white rice, rinsed until water runs clear

½ cup frozen mixed vegetables, such as diced carrots, peas, and corn

6 sprigs fresh cilantro

1. To a small pot, add the chicken stock, tomato paste, salt, and black pepper. While preparing the rice, bring to a simmer over medium heat.

2. In a large pan with a lid, heat the oil, onion, and garlic over medium heat. When the garlic starts to sizzle, add the rice, stirring constantly, and fry until translucent, 4 to 5 minutes.

3. Pour in the warm stock mixture and bring to a boil. Add the mixed vegetables and cilantro, and reduce heat to low; cover with a tight-fitting lid, and cook for 12 minutes.

4. Remove the pan from the heat, and let sit for 10 minutes undisturbed. Remove the lid, fluff the grains with a fork, and serve immediately.

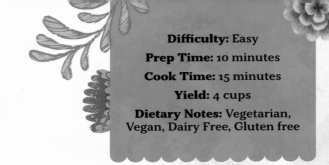

Pasta de Frijol

Avocado Leaf–Infused Bean Paste

Difficulty: Easy
Prep Time: 10 minutes
Cook Time: 15 minutes
Yield: 4 cups
Dietary Notes: Vegetarian, Vegan, Dairy Free, Gluten free

Flavored with spicy dried chiles and the unique anise-like aroma of avocado leaves, this black bean paste can be used as a filling for tamales, huaraches, and empanadas, or spread on a tortilla with crumbled queso. This recipe makes about 4 cups of bean paste.

4 cups cooked black beans

1 dried árbol chile, stemmed

2 dried avocado leaves

2 tablespoons vegetable oil (or other neutral-flavored oil)

¼ white onion, chopped

1. Using a slotted spoon, transfer beans to a blender; reserve the bean broth. Add the árbol chile and avocado leaves to the blender, and purée until smooth, adding only enough reserved bean broth to help "release" the blender blades.

2. Heat oil in a large sauté pan over medium heat, and add the chopped onion. Cook the onion until it just starts to caramelize; then pour in the black bean purée. Fry the beans for 10 to 15 minutes, stirring frequently to prevent them from burning, until the mixture has thickened. Taste and adjust the seasoning, as needed.

Chiles en Escabeche

Pickled Chiles

Difficulty: Easy

Prep Time: 5 minutes (plus at least 4 hours wait time)

Cook Time: 5 minutes

Yield: 4 cups

Dietary Notes: Vegan, Dairy Free, Gluten Free

You'll want to keep a bowl of these pickled chiles in your refrigerator to deliver an exciting new element to your meals.

6 jalapeño chiles, stemmed and sliced into ¼-inch rounds

1 large carrot, peeled and sliced into ¼-inch rounds

½ white onion, thinly sliced

2 garlic cloves

1 dried bay leaf

6 whole cloves

1 teaspoon allspice berries

½ teaspoon dried Mexican oregano

2 cups apple cider vinegar

1 teaspoon kosher salt

6 tablespoons grated piloncillo or dark brown sugar

1. Put the chiles, carrot, onion, and garlic in a heatproof bowl.

2. Warm a saucepan over medium heat, and toast the bay leaf, cloves, allspice, and oregano until fragrant, 20 to 30 seconds. Transfer the toasted spices to the bowl with the chiles while you prepare the vinegar.

3. Put the pan back on medium heat; add the vinegar, salt, and piloncillo, and bring to a steady simmer. Immediately pour the brine over the chiles and toasted spices, and let the mixture cool to room temperature before transferring it to an airtight container in the refrigerator.

4. Let the chiles marinate for at least 4 hours before using them in recipes.

Cebollas Encurtidas

Pickled Onions

Difficulty: Easy
Prep Time: 5 minutes (plus at least 4 hours wait time)
Cook Time: 5 minutes
Yield: 4 cups
Dietary Notes: Vegan, Dairy Free, Gluten Free

These peppery pickled onions add a sharp, zesty flavor to many savory dishes, from cheesy quesadillas to braised meats. For a deeper pickled flavor, let the onions marinate overnight until their color takes on a more uniform and bright pink color.

2 medium red onions, thinly sliced

2 dried árbol chiles, stemmed

3 garlic cloves, smashed

½ teaspoon black peppercorns

1 dried bay leaf

⅛ teaspoon cumin seeds

2 teaspoons coriander seeds

1⅓ cups apple cider vinegar

2 teaspoons kosher salt

2 teaspoons sugar

1. Place sliced onions in a heatproof bowl.

2. Warm a small pot over medium heat. Add the chiles, garlic, peppercorns, bay leaf, cumin, and coriander, and toast until fragrant, about 30 seconds. Add the toasted spices to the bowl with the sliced onions, and let sit while you prepare the vinegar.

3. To the same pot, add the vinegar, salt, and sugar. Bring to a steady simmer over medium-high heat; then immediately pour the brine over the onions. Let the onions cool to room temperature for 1 hour before transferring them to an airtight container.

4. Store the onions in the refrigerator. Let them marinate for at least 4 hours before using them in recipes.

Dulces y Postres

SWEETS AND PASTRIES

Calabaza en Tacha

Candied Winter Squash

Difficulty: Easy
Prep Time: 10 minutes
Cook Time: 30 to 45 minutes
Yield: 8 to 12 servings
Dietary Notes: Vegan, Dairy Free, Gluten Free

Throughout *Coco*, the Rivera family remembers ancestors with family photos and various foods. One of the various foods you might find is calabaza, or winter squash, which are sold by vendors near La Plaza Santa Cecilia in the film. After the holidays, perhaps Abuelita would make this traditional dessert, which features a sticky, caramel-like sweetness that is very easy to love.

4 pounds kabocha, hubbard, or Castilla squash, cut into 4-inch chunks

2 pounds piloncillo or dark brown sugar

2 whole cloves

½ tablespoon anise seeds

One 4-inch stick Mexican cinnamon

¼ cup orange juice

4 to 5 long strips of orange zest

1. Add the squash, skin side down, to a large pot along with 4 cups of water, piloncillo, cloves, anise seed, cinnamon, orange juice, and orange zest. It's okay if some of the squash remains uncovered by water.

2. Bring to a simmer over medium heat; then cover the pot, reduce heat to medium-low, and continue cooking for 30 minutes.

3. The piloncillo and water should form a thick, dark syrup, and the squash should be easily pierced with a toothpick. If the squash is cooked but the syrup has not thickened enough, remove the squash and continue simmering the syrup, uncovered, until it becomes thick.

4. Return the squash to the pot, and coat it evenly in the syrup. Serve warm or at room temperature.

Difficulty: Medium
Prep Time: 15 minutes
Cook Time: 20 minutes
Yield: 12 churros
Dietary Notes: Vegetarian

Churros

Many ancestors return to the Land of the Dead with delicious treats to declare at Marigold Grand Central Station. These cinnamon sugar–dusted delights are easy to spot while waiting in line. Crispy on the outside and soft on the inside, they're so delectable that it's no wonder los muertos come back for them every year.

CHURROS

3 to 4 cups vegetable oil, for frying

1 teaspoon ground cinnamon

¼ cup granulated sugar

1 cup water

1 teaspoon vanilla extract

⅛ teaspoon salt

2 tablespoons butter

1 cup all-purpose flour, sifted

1 large egg, beaten

CHOCOLATE SAUCE

¼ cup heavy cream, plus more if needed

One 3-ounce tablet Mexican chocolate, chopped

1 tablespoon unsalted butter

3 tablespoons unsweetened cocoa powder (optional for thicker chocolate)

¼ teaspoon vanilla extract

¼ teaspoon ground cinnamon

SPECIALTY TOOLS

Pastry bag with star-shape tip

Candy thermometer

TO MAKE THE CHURROS:

1. Using a candy thermometer, preheat the vegetable oil in a large heavy-bottomed pot to 320°F while you make the churro batter. Mix the cinnamon and sugar on a large plate. Set aside.

2. Place the water, vanilla extract, salt, and butter in a saucepan over medium-high heat. When it reaches a rolling boil, stir in the flour all at once and remove the saucepan from the heat. Mix the dough quickly and vigorously, using a wooden spoon or spatula to scrape the sides of the pan. Add the egg; keep mixing until the egg is completely incorporated and you have a smooth, soft dough that comes away from the pot, about 2 to 3 minutes.

3. Place the dough in a pastry bag fitted with a star-shape tip, making sure to squeeze out any air bubbles in the dough. Onto a parchment-lined baking sheet, pipe 6-inch strips of dough until you've used all the dough. Alternatively, you can pipe 6-inch strips of dough directly into the hot oil, cutting them with kitchen scissors.

4. When you add the raw dough to the hot oil, it should bubble rapidly. Fry each churro for about 3 to 4 minutes until golden brown, turning them occasionally for even crispness and color.

5. When the churros are golden all around, remove them from the oil and place them on a paper towel to drain before rolling each churro in the cinnamon-sugar mixture. Set them aside or keep them warm in a 300°F oven while you make the chocolate dipping sauce.

TO MAKE THE CHOCOLATE SAUCE:

6. Heat the heavy cream in medium sauce pot over medium-high heat until it comes to a slow boil. Remove the pan from the heat, and add the chocolate. Let the chocolate sit in the hot cream for 3 to 5 minutes to soften. Then add the butter, cocoa powder (if using), vanilla extract, and ground cinnamon; whisk to incorporate. If the chocolate is too thick, stir in additional cream 1 tablespoon at a time, until it is the desired consistency.

7. Serve the churros with the chocolate sauce in a cup for dipping.

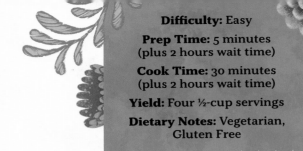

Difficulty: Easy

Prep Time: 5 minutes
(plus 2 hours wait time)

Cook Time: 30 minutes
(plus 2 hours wait time)

Yield: Four ½-cup servings

Dietary Notes: Vegetarian,
Gluten Free

Nicuatole

Oaxacan Corn Flan with Berry Sauce

These flan-like delicacies are traditionally colored bright red with the help of carmine powder, a natural dye made from an insect. The Berry Sauce in this recipe is inspired by the dessert's characteristic shock of red, while also giving the nicuatole a refreshing touch of sweetness.

FLAN

½ cup masa harina

⅓ cup sugar

2 cups whole milk

One 2-inch piece Mexican cinnamon stick

Butter, for greasing

BERRY SAUCE

2 cups frozen red berries, such as raspberries or strawberries

3 tablespoons sugar

1 teaspoon lime juice

TO MAKE THE FLAN:

1. Add the masa, sugar, and milk to a medium pan, and whisk together until the masa is dissolved. Add the cinnamon stick, and heat the mixture over medium-low heat.

2. Stir the masa frequently for 20 to 30 minutes to make sure it doesn't burn to the bottom of the pan. The consistency of the masa starts as a very runny soup and slowly becomes more like a thick pancake batter.

3. Grease small ramekins, molds, or coffee cups, and add the cooked masa. Let the masa cool at room temperature while you make the Berry Sauce.

TO MAKE THE BERRY SAUCE:

4. Add the berries, sugar, and lime juice to a small bowl. Thoroughly mash the berries with a fork or potato masher, and let sit for at least 2 hours or overnight. The fruit mash will look chunkier at first but will continue releasing liquid as it macerates in the sugar and lime juice.

5. To serve, unmold the nicuatole by running a thin, sharp knife around the edges and then turning it out onto a plate. Serve the nicuatole with a couple tablespoons of Berry Sauce drizzled over the top.

6. Store the nicuatole in an airtight container in the refrigerator for up to 5 days. The Berry Sauce can be stored in a lidded jar in the refrigerator for up to a week or can be frozen for several months.

Alegría
Popped Amaranth Candy

These puffed seed candies are a perfect balance of sweet and nutty. They will have you singing, "*Señoras y señores*, to be here with you tonight brings me joy, *que alegría!*"

⅔ cup uncooked amaranth seeds, divided

¼ cup raw, hulled pepitas

½ cup honey

½ teaspoon kosher salt

½ teaspoon ground cinnamon

⅛ teaspoon lime juice

SPECIALTY TOOLS

Candy thermometer

1. To puff the amaranth seeds, warm medium sauce pot with a glass lid over medium heat. Set a fine-mesh strainer over a bowl, and put aside.

2. Test the heat by sprinkling water in the pan with your fingers—if the water sizzles immediately, the pan is ready. Add a tablespoon of amaranth seeds at a time, and cover with the lid. The seeds should start popping immediately. Keep moving the pan while the seeds are popping, about 10 to 15 seconds. Transfer the seeds to the strainer, and shake out the unpopped seeds. Repeat step 2 with the remaining amaranth seeds.

3. Discard the unpopped amaranth seeds, and transfer the puffed amaranth and pepitas to the bowl. Set aside.

4. In a small pot, add the honey and salt, and cook over medium-high heat until the honey starts to foam. Immediately reduce heat to low, and simmer until the honey reaches 300°F using a candy thermometer.

5. Remove the honey from the heat, and stir in the cinnamon and lime juice. Pour the honey into the puffed amaranth and pepitas, and quickly stir to combine. Transfer to the center of a greased baking sheet, and cover with a piece of parchment paper.

6. Using a rolling pin, roll out the mixture to 1 inch thick. Let cool, and cut into desired shapes using a sharp knife or cookie cutters.

7. Store the alegría in an airtight container at room temperature for up to a week.

Difficulty: Easy
Prep Time: 10 minutes
Cook Time: 10 minutes
Yield: About 20 small bars
Dietary Notes: Vegetarian, Dairy Free, Gluten Free

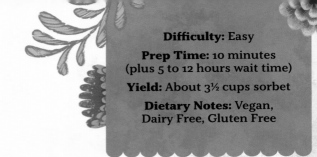

Mango Sorbet with Chamoy

Difficulty: Easy

Prep Time: 10 minutes
(plus 5 to 12 hours wait time)

Yield: About 3½ cups sorbet

Dietary Notes: Vegan,
Dairy Free, Gluten Free

Fruteros (fruit vendors) are skilled artists who carve beautifully delicate flowers out of mangoes. When the masterpiece is complete, they drizzle *chamoy* over the top to balance the mango's sweetness with a salty and spicy kick. Save yourself countless hours becoming a fruit flower artist by making this easy mango sorbet in a fraction of the time.

SORBET

4 large ripe mangoes, peeled and cut off the pit, or 4 cups frozen mango pieces, thawed

⅓ cup sugar or ¼ cup light corn syrup

⅓ cup water

⅓ cup freshly squeezed lime juice

⅛ teaspoon kosher salt

¼ cup strawberry jam or Chamoy (recipe follows)

Ancho chile powder, to garnish

CHAMOY

1 cup dried apricots

½ cup prunes, seeded, or ¼ cup raisins

½ cup dried hibiscus flowers

7 dried árbol chiles, stemmed and seeded

3 tablespoons chile powder or Tajín, plus more to taste

¼ cup sugar

¼ cup lime juice

¼ teaspoon kosher salt

SPECIALTY TOOLS

Ice cream maker

NOTES

You can add the jam and chile powder to the ice cream maker and mix it in loosely with a spatula, to make swirls before freezing.

TO MAKE THE SORBET:

1. Add the mangoes to a blender or food processor, and purée until smooth. Measure the purée to be sure you have 3 to 3½ cups of mango purée.

2. Transfer the mango purée to a large mixing bowl. Add the sugar, water, lime juice, and salt, and stir until the sugar dissolves. Chill the puréed mango mixture in the refrigerator for at least 2 hours, preferably overnight.

3. Remove the mango purée, and churn it according to the instructions provided for your ice cream maker. This can take approximately 20 minutes. The texture of the sorbet should be similar to soft serve—not too hard or runny.

4. Transfer the sorbet to a container to store, and freeze for at least 3 hours. When ready to serve, remove the sorbet from the freezer and let it sit for 20 to 30 minutes.

TO MAKE THE CHAMOY:

5. To a medium saucepan, add the apricots, prunes, flowers, chiles, 1 tablespoon chile powder or Tajín, and sugar. Bring to a boil over high heat; then reduce the heat to low, and simmer for 30 minutes. Turn off heat and let the mixture sit until completely cooled, at least 1 hour. Taste and add more chile powder to Tajín as desired.

6. Add the mixture to a blender, add lime juice and salt, and purée. If the mixture is too pasty and thick, add 1 to 2 tablespoons of water until you're able to drizzle it nicely.

7. Transfer to a quart-size jar with a lid, and store in the refrigerator for up to 2 months.

8. To serve: Portion the sorbet into bowls; then spoon 1 tablespoon of jam or chamoy over the sorbet and add a sprinkling of chile powder, to taste.

Mexican Chocolate Popcorn

Difficulty: Easy
Prep Time: 5 minutes
Cook Time: 55 minutes
Yield: 7 cups popcorn
Dietary Notes: Vegetarian, Gluten Free, Contains Nut Extract

Popcorn and chocolate are ancient foods that can be traced back thousands of years to present-day Mexico. Lightly spiced with cinnamon and almond to conjure the flavors of Mexican chocolate, this addictive snack goes perfectly with the talent competition in La Plaza Santa Cecilia in the film, the Sunrise Spectacular, or a cozy movie night at home.

4 tablespoons unsalted butter, plus more for greasing

7 cups freshly popped popcorn

⅓ cup light corn syrup

1 cup sugar

¼ teaspoon kosher salt

3 ounces 72% dark chocolate, chopped finely

¼ teaspoon ground cinnamon

1 teaspoon almond extract

¾ teaspoon baking soda

1. Move the oven rack to the middle position, and preheat the oven to 250°F. Line a baking sheet with aluminum foil, and grease with butter or oil spray.

2. Place the freshly popped popcorn in a large mixing bowl, and set aside.

3. To a large pan, add the butter, corn syrup, sugar, salt, and ⅓ cup water. Bring to a boil over high heat. Reduce heat to medium-low, and cook, stirring constantly, with a rubber spatula until the sugar dissolves and the mixture is smooth, 3 to 5 minutes.

4. Turn off the heat. Stir in the chocolate, cinnamon, and almond extract until the chocolate is melted; then immediately add the baking soda. When the chocolate sauce is foamy, pour it over the popcorn and quickly coat the popcorn.

5. Scrape the popcorn onto the prepared baking sheet, and level it with the spatula in an even single layer. Bake the popcorn for 20 minutes; remove the pan and carefully stir the popcorn.

6. Level the popcorn again in an even single layer; then put it back in the oven to continue baking for another 30 minutes until the chocolate coating forms a crispy shell.

7. Remove the popcorn from the oven and stir one more time. Let it cool completely in the pan before serving.

Pan Dulce

SWEET BREADS

Difficulty: Advanced
Prep Time: 1 hour
(plus 1 hour wait time)
Cook Time: 20 to 40 minutes
Yield: 12 conchas
Dietary Notes: Vegetarian

Concha

When Miguel is brought to the Department of Family Reunions, the clerk who helps him is snacking on one of these delicious sweet breads. While he's explaining how Miguel is cursed because he robbed a grave, Miguel's companion, Dante, tries to eat the *concha* when no one's looking. You'll love these pillowy-soft conchas that are beloved on both sides of the Marigold Bridge—just be sure to keep an eye on your plate, in case someone else tries to sneak away with it!

CONCHA

1 tablespoon active dry yeast

1 teaspoon plus 7 tablespoons sugar, divided

½ cup warm water

½ cup warm whole milk

1 teaspoon kosher salt

2 eggs, at room temperature

2 teaspoons vanilla extract

4 cups all-purpose flour, plus more for dusting

18 tablespoons unsalted butter, softened, divided, plus more for greasing

VANILLA TOPPING

1½ cups confectioner's sugar

1½ cups all-purpose flour

1 cup butter

1 tablespoon vanilla extract

Pinch of kosher salt

CHOCOLATE TOPPING

1½ cups confectioner's sugar

1½ cups all-purpose flour

1 cup butter

1 teaspoon vanilla extract

3 tablespoons cocoa powder

Pinch of kosher salt

SPECIALTY TOOLS

Shell mold (optional)

TO MAKE THE CONCHA:

1. In the bowl of a stand mixer, whisk together the yeast and 1 tablespoon of sugar, then add the warm water and warm milk. Let the mixture sit until it starts to bubble, 10 minutes.

2. Add the remaining sugar, salt, eggs, vanilla, and flour; mix on medium speed using a dough hook, about 10 minutes.

3. Add 13 tablespoons butter to the mixture a couple tablespoons at a time until fully incorporated. Raise the speed to medium, and continue mixing until the dough pulls away from the sides of the bowl and forms a smooth, elastic-looking ball around the hook, 10 more minutes.

4. Butter a large mixing bowl, and transfer the dough to the bowl. Cover the bowl with plastic wrap, and let it sit in a warm spot until it doubles in size, 1 hour.

Continued on page 106

Continued from page 105

5. Line three 13-by-18-inch rimmed baking sheets with parchment paper or a silicone mat. Lightly dust a clean countertop with flour, and transfer the dough to the floured surface. Using a bench scraper, portion the dough into about 14 balls, each one about 2½ ounces or ⅓ cup. One by one, pat down the portioned dough into a flat shape; then bring the edges of the dough to the center, to form a ball.

6. Turn a dough ball onto a clean work surface. Cupping lightly with your hand, move your hand in circles to form a neater, tighter ball of dough. Repeat with the remaining dough balls. Place the balls on a prepared baking sheet, leaving about 2 inches between each one so they don't stick together as they rise. Cover the dough balls with a clean dish towel, and leave them on a counter to rest while making the topping.

TO MAKE THE VANILLA TOPPING:

7. Add the confectioner's sugar, flour, butter, vanilla, and salt to the bowl of a stand mixer. Using the paddle attachment, mix on low speed to combine before gradually working up to medium speed. The mixture should be smooth and look like cookie dough. On a clean work surface, place a large sheet of parchment paper and then transfer the vanilla dough to the parchment. Place another large sheet of parchment paper on top of the dough; then use a rolling pin to roll out the dough to ⅛-inch thickness. Remove the top piece of parchment paper and punch out circles using a 3-inch cookie cutter.

TO MAKE THE CHOCOLATE TOPPING:

8. Add the confectioner's sugar, flour, butter, vanilla extract, cocoa powder, and salt to the bowl of a stand mixer. Using the paddle attachment, mix on low speed to combine before gradually working up to medium speed. The mixture should be smooth and look like cookie dough. On a clean work surface, place a large sheet of parchment paper and then transfer the chocolate dough to the parchment. Place another large sheet of parchment paper on top of the dough; then use a rolling pin to roll out the dough to ⅛-inch thickness. Remove the top piece of parchment paper and punch out circles using a 3-inch cookie cutter.

9. With the remaining 5 tablespoons butter, lightly brush butter over each of the concha balls over each of the concha balls and place a round vanilla or chocolate topping disk on top of each concha, carefully adhering the disks to the concha. The topping should be about ¼ inch away from touching the bottom of the pan. Repeat with the remaining topping dough.

10. Preheat the oven to 375°F. If you're using a shell mold, lightly dip the mold in flour; then gently press the mold onto the topping and roll it from one side to the other in a swift, nonstop motion. Don't push too hard: It will pierce the dough or cause the topping to break apart when baking. You can also leave the topping as is, without any design.

11. Bake the conchas until golden brown and puffed up, about 20 minutes. If the three sheet pans don't all fit in the oven at the same time, you can bake one or two at a time.

12. Let the conchas rest for a few minutes before enjoying. Conchas can be stored in an airtight container for up to four days but are best enjoyed the same day.

Difficulty: Easy
Prep Time: 20 minutes
Cook Time: 20 to 25 minutes
Yield: One 9-by-13-inch cake
Dietary Notes: Vegetarian

Cortadillo

This is a classic pan dulce that children simply can't get enough of, which might explain its other name, *Pastel de Niños* (Children's Cake). This pink cake is also eaten by the clerk in the Department of Family Reunions and even security guards at the Sunrise Spectacular, proving that it can be enjoyed at any age and in any world.

CAKE

2¼ cups cake flour

¼ cup corn flour, sifted

2½ teaspoons baking powder

½ teaspoon kosher salt

¾ cup unsalted butter, softened

1 cup sugar

2 teaspoons vanilla extract

Finely grated zest of 1 lemon or ½ orange (about 1 tablespoon)

3 eggs

1 cup whole milk

PINK FROSTING

1 cup unsalted butter, softened

1 teaspoon vanilla extract

½ teaspoon kosher salt

Finely grated zest of 1 lemon (about 1 tablespoon)

4 cups confectioner's sugar, sifted

¼ cup heavy cream

Red food coloring

Nonpareil sprinkles

TO MAKE THE CAKE:

1. Preheat the oven to 350°F, and move the oven rack to the middle position. Line a 9-by-13-inch baking dish with parchment paper, and set aside.

2. In a medium mixing bowl, whisk together the cake flour, corn flour, baking powder, and salt; set aside.

3. In the bowl of a stand mixer with the paddle attachment, cream the butter and sugar on medium speed for about 2 minutes until the butter looks fluffy and very light in color.

4. Mix in the vanilla and lemon or orange zest; then mix in one egg at a time, fully incorporating it before adding another egg.

5. Turn down the speed to low, and mix in ⅓ of the flour mixture, followed by ⅓ of the milk. Continue adding the flour and milk in phases until the batter is a smooth, uniform consistency.

6. Scrape down the sides of the bowl with a silicone spatula; then pour the batter into the prepared baking dish. Smooth out the surface, and bake for 20 to 25 minutes until the cake is golden brown and a toothpick inserted into the center of the cake comes out clean. Let the cake cool completely before adding the frosting.

TO MAKE THE PINK FROSTING:

7. In the bowl of a stand mixer with the paddle attachment, cream the butter, vanilla, salt, and lemon zest for 1 minute at medium-high speed. Turn down the speed to low, and add the confectioner's sugar ½ cup at a time. When all the sugar is incorporated, add the heavy cream. Increase the speed slowly to medium-high, and beat for 1 minute until the frosting is very light and fluffy. Add a couple drops of food coloring, and mix on low just to combine. Add any additional food coloring a drop at a time until the color is a deep pink.

8. With a silicone spatula, spread the frosting evenly over the top of the cake, and add the sprinkles while the frosting is still slightly wet. Let the frosting dry completely before you cut the cake.

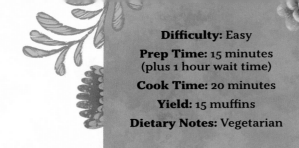

Difficulty: Easy
Prep Time: 15 minutes
(plus 1 hour wait time)
Cook Time: 20 minutes
Yield: 15 muffins
Dietary Notes: Vegetarian

Mantecada

In *Coco*, rainbow hued and finely designed *papel picado* decorate the streets of Santa Cecilia for all the special fiestas. It's easy to be charmed by their colors, and the same is true with these buttery muffins. When making this pan dulce, be sure to rest the dough in the refrigerator so that it becomes fluffy when baked.

2 cups all-purpose flour

1¼ teaspoons baking powder

1 teaspoon baking soda

1 teaspoon kosher salt

½ teaspoon ground cinnamon

1 cup buttermilk

Finely grated zest of 1 orange
(about 2 tablespoons)

3 eggs

2 teaspoons vanilla extract

½ cup butter or vegetable shortening,
at room temperature

1 cup sugar

15 multicolored cupcake liners

1. Sift together the flour, baking powder, baking soda, salt, and cinnamon into a small mixing bowl. In another small mixing bowl, whisk the buttermilk, orange zest, eggs, and vanilla extract.

2. In the bowl of a stand mixer with the paddle attachment, whip together the butter and sugar until very fluffy and pale, about 2 minutes. Add half of the dry ingredients mixture, and mix until incorporated; then add half the wet ingredients mixture. Repeat until you've used all the dry and wet ingredients. Stop the mixer as needed to scrape down the sides of the bowl with a silicone spatula.

3. When all ingredients are fully incorporated, cover the batter and let rest in the refrigerator for at least 1 hour.

4. Remove the batter from the refrigerator. Preheat your oven to 400°F.

5. Line a muffin pan with the cupcake liners. Using a tablespoon or cookie scoop, add 3 tablespoons of batter to each of the cupcake liners, or two 1½-tablespoon cookie scoops.

6. Bake for 5 minutes; then lower the oven temperature to 350°F, and continue baking for an additional 15 minutes.

7. The *mantecadas* are finished cooking when a toothpick inserted into the center comes out clean. Store in an airtight container at room temperature for up to 4 days.

> NOTE
>
> Papel picado is a traditional Mexican folk art featuring cut paper banners in many different shapes, sizes, and colors. It is commonly used for holidays, special events, and celebrations.

Polvorones

Difficulty: Easy
Prep Time: 20 minutes
(plus 1 hour wait time)
Cook Time: 50 minutes
Yield: About 16 cookies
Dietary Notes: Vegetarian,
Contains Nuts

When people learned the truth about Ernesto de la Cruz, his reputation and career became like one of these cookies—in crumbles. These delicious shortbread-like treats are so delicate that they melt in your mouth. No one is able to eat just one!

½ cup raw almonds or pecans

4 cups cake flour

¾ teaspoon baking powder

¾ teaspoon kosher salt

¼ cup sugar

¾ teaspoon ground cinnamon

Finely grated zest of 1 orange

1 cup unsalted butter (2 sticks), melted

1 teaspoon vanilla extract

Confectioner's sugar, for dusting

1. Preheat the oven to 350°F. Add the almonds to a small baking sheet, and spread the flour evenly on a separate baking sheet. Toast the almonds for about 10 minutes. Toast the flour until it is a deeper cream color, about 20 minutes. Remove and set aside to cool completely before moving on to the next step.

2. Sift the cooled flour, baking powder, and salt into a medium mixing bowl, and set aside. To a food processor, combine the toasted almonds, sugar, cinnamon, and orange zest; process until the almonds are ground but still somewhat chunky.

3. Transfer the ground nuts mixture to a stand mixer with a paddle attachment, and beat in the melted butter and vanilla on low speed. Add in the toasted flour, and mix until just incorporated on low speed. The dough should be crumbly, like pie crust dough.

4. Portion a larger piece of plastic wrap on a clean board or counter, and transfer the dough to the center of the plastic. Gather the edges of the plastic wrap, and very lightly press the dough together until it forms a disk. Rest the dough in a cool place for 1 hour.

5. When ready to bake, preheat the oven again to 350°F. Line a large baking sheet with parchment paper. Using a small cookie or ice cream scoop, scoop out leveled dough onto the pans, leaving at least 1 inch of space between each dough ball. Bake the cookies until they are a pale golden color, 25 to 30 minutes, turning the pan about halfway through.

6. When the cookies are out of the oven, dust them with confectioner's sugar and set them aside to cool completely. *Polvorones* can be stored for several days at room temperature in an airtight container.

Difficulty: Advanced
Prep Time: 1 hour
(plus 3 hours wait time)
Cook Time: 20 to 25 minutes
Yield: 8 breads
Dietary Notes: Vegetarian

Pan de Muerto

This iconic sweet bread is customarily left for the ancestors as nourishment for the journey back across the Marigold Bridge. Many types of *Pan de Muerto* are made—some have small figurines partially tucked into the bread to resemble a coffin, whereas others are painted with intricate designs. This "skull and bones" design is the most well-known. Their distinct sweetness comes from anise and orange blossom, which pairs perfectly with warm Champurrado (page 123).

½ cup warm whole milk

1 tablespoon active dry yeast

1 cup plus 7 tablespoons sugar, divided

3 eggs, at room temperature

1¼ teaspoons kosher salt

1 teaspoon grated orange zest

1 teaspoon orange blossom water

3 cups all-purpose flour

¼ teaspoon ground anise

1 cup plus 1 tablespoon unsalted butter, softened, divided, plus more for greasing

1. In the bowl of a stand mixer, whisk together the milk, yeast, and 1 teaspoon sugar. Let the mixture sit until it starts to bubble, 10 minutes.

2. In another small bowl, whisk together the eggs, 6 tablespoons of sugar, salt, orange zest, and orange blossom water.

3. To the milk mixture, add the egg mixture, flour, and ground anise, and mix together until a shaggy dough forms. Attach the bowl to the stand mixer and, using the dough hook attachment, start adding 14 tablespoons of butter, 1 tablespoon at a time, on medium-low speed. Add the next tablespoon of butter only after the previous one is fully incorporated.

4. Scrape down the sides of the bowl, as needed. When all 14 tablespoons of butter have been added, increase the speed to medium and beat for another 10 minutes, until the dough pulls away from the sides of the bowl and forms a smooth, elastic ball around the hook.

5. Butter a mixing bowl, and transfer the dough to the bowl. Cover the bowl with plastic wrap; let it sit in a warm place until it doubles in size, about 1 hour.

6. Gently deflate the dough: Lift up one side of the dough and fold it one-third of the way across the dough; then lift the opposite side of the dough and fold it one-third across the dough the other way. Turn over the dough so that the bottom is now the top, cover it again with plastic wrap, and let it rest while you make the decorations.

Continued on page 113

Continued from page 111

7. Line two baking sheets with parchment paper or silicone baking mats, and grease with extra butter or cooking spray. Turn out the dough onto a clean and lightly floured work surface. Divide the dough into eight equal pieces; then tear off a tablespoon-size piece from each of the dough balls and set them aside. Reshape the eight larger doughs into balls, and space them evenly apart on a prepared baking sheet. From the eight tablespoon-size pieces, pinch off a teaspoon-size piece and roll into a smooth round ball. Place in a single row on the prepared baking sheet, about 1 inch apart. These are the "skulls."

8. With the remaining small pieces of dough, divide each in half so that you now have sixteen small pieces of dough. To make the "crossbones" for the bread, roll the small piece into a thin rope about 3 inches long, using the palm of your hand. Pinch the rope at the middle and then once on both sides of the middle so that the rope now looks like joints. Carefully transfer the "bones" to another prepared baking sheet, and repeat with the remaining dough. Loosely cover both pans with greased plastic wrap or a clean dish towel, and let the dough rest until it has doubled in size, about 1 hour.

9. Lightly flatten one of the large dough balls, and brush with softened butter. Place two of the "bone" pieces on top of the dough, crossing them to form an X; then press them into the dough. Using 1 tablespoon butter, brush a little bit in the center. in the center where the bones overlap; then place the "skull" in the middle, pressing down lightly to secure it. Repeat with the remaining dough. Cover the pieces with greased plastic wrap or a dish towel, and let them rest for an hour.

10. Move the oven rack to the middle position, and preheat to 350°F. Uncover the dough and place in the oven to bake for 20 to 25 minutes until it is a deep golden brown color. Transfer the breads to a wire rack, and let them cool completely.

11. When the breads are cooled, melt the remaining 2 tablespoons of butter, brush the breads with butter. With the remaining sugar, sprinkle a generous amount over the tops of the breads.

12. Let the breads cool before serving. Wrap leftover pieces tightly, and store at room temperature for up to 5 days.

Difficulty: Easy
Prep Time: 20 minutes
(plus 1 hour wait time)
Cook Time: 20 minutes
Yield: 8 cookie sandwiches
Dietary Notes: Vegetarian

Besos

Buttery cookies are filled with fruit jam or caramel and then pressed together until they kiss, which is where this pan dulce gets its name. After they are rolled in coconut, they are a perfect treat to share with loved ones—and a fitting end to any journey.

14 tablespoons (1¾ sticks) butter, softened

1 cup plus 2 tablespoons sugar

2 eggs

3 cups all-purpose flour

1 tablespoon baking powder

1 teaspoon kosher salt

½ cup whole milk

2 teaspoons vanilla extract

Finely grated zest of 1 lemon (about 1 tablespoon)

1 cup fruit jam, dulce de leche, or *cajeta*

2 cups unsweetened finely shredded coconut flakes

1. Preheat the oven to 350°F. Prepare a large baking sheet with parchment paper or a silicone baking mat.

2. Cream the butter and sugar in the bowl of a stand mixer with the paddle attachment until it's light in color and fluffy, 3 to 4 minutes.

3. Add the eggs one at a time until incorporated; add the flour, baking powder, and salt, and continue to beat on low speed.

4. In a separate bowl, whisk together the milk, vanilla extract, and lemon zest. Add them to the mixing bowl of the stand mixer, and continue beating on low speed until well incorporated.

5. With slightly damp hands, portion 2 tablespoons of batter per cookie, and form balls. You can use a similarly sized cookie or ice cream scoop to portion the batter.

6. Place the balls on a baking sheet with 1 inch of space between each one. Bake for 20 minutes or until the bottoms of the cookies are golden. Remove the cookies from the oven and let them cool completely.

7. To assemble, separate out half of the cookies. Place 1 tablespoon of jam or other filling on the flat side of the cookie, and spread evenly. Place another cookie on top of the jam, to make a little sandwich. Add the coconut flakes to a small bowl; brush a thin layer of jam over the *besos*, and roll the cookies in the coconut flakes.

8. Let the besos dry on a wire rack for at least 1 hour before enjoying them.

Bebidas

BEVERAGES

Agua de Jamaica

Hibiscus Flower Water

Difficulty: Easy

Prep Time: 10 minutes (plus wait time)

Cook Time: 5 minutes

Yield: 2 quarts

Dietary Notes: Vegan, Dairy Free, Gluten Free

The drink stands in *Coco*'s La Plaza Santa Cecilia sell these fruity refreshers from large clear jugs, with all their vibrant colors on full display. They are the perfect refresher to have when you're watching the mariachi play in the talent contest (just don't tell Abuelita that you were there).

1½ cups dried hibiscus flowers

⅔ cup sugar

Juice of 1 lime (about 1 tablespoon)

1. Rinse the dried hibiscus flowers under cold water in a strainer, to remove all dust and grit.

2. In a medium pot over high heat, bring 2 quarts (8 cups) of water to a boil. Add the rinsed flowers and sugar, stirring to dissolve the sugar; then turn off the heat and let steep for 30 minutes. When cooled to room temperature, the flowers will fall to the bottom of the pot.

3. Strain the hibiscus water into a pitcher, and stir in the lime juice. Refrigerate the drink until it is cold. Serve over ice, adjusting the sugar or lime juice to suit your taste.

Agua de Limón con Chía

Lime Water with Chia Seeds

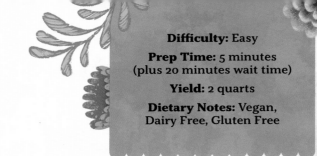

Difficulty: Easy
Prep Time: 5 minutes
(plus 20 minutes wait time)
Yield: 2 quarts
Dietary Notes: Vegan,
Dairy Free, Gluten Free

Kids such as Miguel love this *agua* because the chia seeds expand and take on a chewy, tapioca type of texture when soaked in the fruit juice. Mix everything together, and then add more sugar or lime juice, to your liking.

Juice of 8 to 10 limes (about 1 cup)

½ cup sugar

2 tablespoons chia seeds

1. Add 7 cups of water and the lime juice, sugar, and chia seeds to a pitcher. Mix until the sugar is dissolved.

2. Refrigerate the juice for at least 20 minutes, to let the chia seeds hydrate and expand. Serve over ice, adjusting the sugar or lime juice to fit your taste.

Horchata

Rice and Almond Milk with Cinnamon

Difficulty: Easy
Prep Time: 10 minutes
(plus 2 to 12 hours wait time)
Cook Time: 5 minutes
Yield: 6 cups
Dietary Notes: Vegan,
Dairy Free, Contains Nuts,
Gluten Free

Rice and almonds give this classic agua a satisfyingly creamy and frothy texture. Spiked with sweet and floral Mexican cinnamon and a splash of vanilla, it's a perfect companion to spicier foods, such as the Birria de Res (page 77) and Barbacoa de Pollo (page 61) that may have been served at Santa Cecilia's very own Tortillería in the film. In some parts of Mexico, horchata is topped with chopped summer fruits and nuts.

1 cup uncooked long-grain white rice

1 cup raw almonds

One 3-inch Mexican cinnamon stick

½ teaspoon kosher salt

3 cups boiling water,
plus 3 cups cold water, divided

⅓ to ½ cup sugar

1 teaspoon vanilla extract

1. To a heatproof container, add rice, almonds, cinnamon stick, salt, and 3 cups of boiling water. Leave uncovered at room temperature for at least 2 hours, but preferably overnight. The longer the rice mixture sits, the deeper the flavor will be.

2. After the rice has softened, add the entire mixture to a blender along with 3 cups of cold water, the sugar, and the vanilla. Blend the mixture on the blender's highest setting for at least 2 minutes until it is very smooth.

3. Pass the blended rice mixture through a fine-mesh strainer or cheesecloth into a pitcher. Serve well chilled over ice.

Champurrado

Corn-Thickened Mexican Hot Chocolate

Difficulty: Easy
Prep Time: 5 minutes
Cook Time: 20 minutes
Yield: About 1 quart
Dietary Notes: Vegetarian, Gluten Free

A warm mug of this rich, silky chocolate beverage is just what you'll want after setting up holiday decorations and while awaiting a visit from the ancestors. The trick to getting a silky-smooth texture for this popular drink is making sure the masa is fully mixed before cooking it.

One 3-inch Mexican cinnamon stick

10 tablespoons masa harina for tortillas

5½ ounces Mexican chocolate

1 to 2 tablespoons grated piloncillo (or dark brown sugar)

1 pinch kosher salt

1. Bring 1¼ cups of water and the cinnamon stick to a boil in a medium sauce pot over medium-high heat. Let simmer for a few minutes, to infuse the water with the cinnamon.

2. While the water simmers, make the masa paste. Add ¾ cup of warm water to a small bowl, and sprinkle in the masa a little at a time, whisking constantly until it forms a smooth, thick paste. If the masa is clumpy, pass the mixture through a fine-mesh strainer.

3. Add the masa paste to the simmering water, and immediately whisk until fully incorporated. Lower the heat to medium, and cook until it is thick and bubbly, about 5 minutes.

4. Add 1 cup of water, the chocolate, piloncillo, and salt, stirring constantly and scraping the bottom of the pan, until the masa is fully cooked and thickened.

5. Remove the cinnamon stick. Serve warm in mugs. If you are reheating, add more water or milk to thin it out, and warm over low heat.

ATOLES

Champurrado is a kind of *atole*, a corn-thickened warm beverage that's been enjoyed in Mesoamerica for thousands of years. It can be prepared simply with masa and water, or flavored with ingredients such as peanuts, pecans, oranges, strawberries, and vanilla.

Ponche

Warm Spiced Fruit Punch

Difficulty: Easy
Prep Time: 5 minutes
Cook Time: 20 minutes
Yield: About 3 quarts
Dietary Notes: Vegan, Dairy Free, Gluten Free

The intoxicating aroma of *ponche* during the fall season makes it one of the best times of the year. This hot, fruit-sweetened drink includes many ingredients you could likely find in *Coco*'s Santa Cecilia mercado, such as apples, quinces, oranges, tamarind, and guavas. If you can't find the ingredients fresh or preserved at your local Latino or Asian markets, you can simply omit them and still enjoy a delightful beverage.

4 ounces piloncillo, about ½ cone

⅓ cup dried hibiscus flowers, rinsed well under cold water

2 tamarind pods, seeded and skinned

1 apple, cubed

1 quince, peeled, cored, and cubed (or 1 pear, cubed)

1 orange, sliced

One 1-inch Mexican cinnamon stick

¼ cup raisins

½ cup pitted prunes

8 tejocotes, peeled and cored (optional)

Three 5-inch pieces of fresh sugar cane, cut into 1-inch pieces (optional)

3 to 4 guavas, cubed

½ cup sugar

1. In a large pot, bring 3 quarts of water to a boil over high heat. Lower the heat to medium; then add the piloncillo, hibiscus, tamarind, apple, quince or pear, orange slices, cinnamon, raisins, prunes, *tejocotes*, and sugar cane to the pot.

2. Cover the pot. Simmer for 20 minutes for slightly crunchier fruit or for 30 minutes for softer fruit. Stir in the cubed guava and sugar, and turn off the heat. Ladle warm ponche and cubed fruits in mugs to serve.

WHAT IS TEJOCOTE?

This cherry tomato–size fruit is most commonly used in ponche. For many years, it wasn't allowed into the United States from Mexico, so ponche makers and drinkers used jarred and preserved tejocote. These days, the fruit is grown locally and becoming more available at Latin markets.

DIETARY CONSIDERATIONS

V: Vegetarian | V+: Vegan | DF: Dairy-Free | GF: Gluten-Free

Ensaladas y Antojitos

Xec: V, DF, GF

Garden Salad with Creamy Pepita Dressing: V, GF

Shredded Carrot and Beet Salad: V, DF, GF

Ensalada de Nopal: V, GF

Papaya with Coconut and Chile: V, GF

Elote Callejero: V, GF

Vuelve a la Vida: DF

Masa

Tortillas de Maíz: V, V+, DF, GF

Roasted Squash Flautas with Red Chile Crema and Salsa Verde: V, GF

Grilled Fish Tacos with Cilantro-Lime Crema and Cabbage Salad: GF

Grilled Steak Tacos with Chorizo Pinto Beans: DF, GF

Quesadillas con Hongos: V, GF

Enchiladas Mineras: V, GF

Enchiladas Suizas: GF

Chilaquiles: V, DF

Huaraches: V, V+, DF, GF

Tamales Salados: DF, GF

Tamal de Chocolate: V, GF

Tamal de Fresa: V, GF

Platos Fuertes

Acelgas con Garbanzo: V, V+, DF, GF

Tortitas de Papa: V

Rajas con Crema: V, GF

Chiles Rellenos: V

Camarones a la Diabla: GF

Barbacoa de Pollo: DF, GF

Tinga de Pollo y Chorizo: DF, GF

Picadillo: DF, GF, Contains Nuts

Pollo Adobado: DF, GF

Pollo en Mole Rojo: DF, Contains Nuts

Albóndigas al Chipotle: DF

Pozole Rojo: DF, GF

Cerdo en Mole Verde: DF, GF

Chicharrones en Salsa Verde: DF, GF

Sopa de Milpa: V, GF

Birria de Res: DF, GF

Sopa de Tortilla: V, V+, DF, GF

Guarniciones

Frijoles de la Olla: V, V+, DF, GF

Arroz Blanco: V, V+, DF, GF

Arroz Rojo: V, V+, DF, GF

Pasta de Frijol: V, V+, DF, GF

Chiles en Escabeche: V, V+, DF, GF

Cebollas Encurtidas: V, V+, DF, GF

Dulces y Postres

Calabaza en Tacha: V, V+, DF, GF

Churros: V

Nicuatole: V, GF

Alegría: V, DF, GF

Mango Sorbet with Chamoy: V, V+, DF, GF

Mexican Chocolate Popcorn: GF, Contains Nut Extract

Pan Dulce

Concha: V

Cortadillo: V

Mantecada: V

Polvorones: V, Contains Nuts

Pan de Muerto: V

Besos: V

Bebidas

Agua de Jamaica: V, V+, DF, GF

Agua de Límon con Chía: V, V+, DF, GF

Horchata: V, V+, DF, GF, Contains Nuts

Champurrado: V, GF

Ponche: V, V+, DF, GF

ABOUT THE AUTHOR

Gino Garcia is a culinary instructor, recipe developer, chef, and food ethnographer based in the Land of the Living—specifically, in Seattle, Washington. His expertise and area of interest is in the regional cuisines, cultures, and histories of Mexico and Latin America. Gino has hosted pop-up events and teaches Mexican cooking classes. Before entering the food world, he worked in the public health sector, focusing on issues related to improving nutrition and food justice outcomes in immigrant and BIPOC communities.

Although he has watched *Coco* dozens of times, Gino cries every single time and continues to fall deeper in love with this film. You can find him on social media @MextizoPNW and at his website, MextizoPNW.com.

ACKNOWLEDGMENTS

Muchísimas gracias to my family—biological and chosen—who support me on my ongoing journey to reconnect. Thank you for reminding me that we are our ancestors' wildest dreams.

TITAN
BOOKS

144 Southwark Street
London SE1 0UP
www.titanbooks.com

 Find us on Facebook: www.facebook.com/TitanBooks
 Follow us on Twitter: @TitanBooks

© 2023 Disney/Pixar

Published by Titan Books, London, in 2023.

A CIP catalogue record for this title is available from the British Library.

ISBN: 9781803364889

Publisher: Raoul Goff
VP, Co-Publisher: Vanessa Lopez
VP, Creative: Chrissy Kwasnik
VP, Manufacturing: Alix Nicholaeff
VP, Group Managing Editor: Vicki Jaeger
Publishing Director: Jamie Thompson
Designer: Brooke McCullum
Editor: Anna Wostenberg
Editorial Assistant: Sami Alvarado
Managing Editor: Maria Spano
Senior/Production Editor: Katie Rokakis
Production Associate: Deena Hashem
Senior Production Manager, Subsidiary Rights: Lina s Palma-Temena

Photographer: Ted Thomas
Food and Prop Stylist: Elena
Food Stylist Assistants: Lauren Tedeschi and August Craig

Insight Editions, in association with Roots of Peace, will plant two trees for each tree used in the manufacturing of this
book. Roots of Peace is an internationally renowned humanitarian organization dedicated to eradicating land mines
worldwide and converting war-torn lands into productive farms and wildlife habitats. Roots of Peace will plant two million
fruit and nut trees in Afghanistan and provide farmers there with the skills and support necessary for sustainable land use.

Manufactured in China by Insight Editions

10 9 8 7 6 5 4 3 2 1